HENLE LATIN STUDY GUIDE

S0-CFD-903

A Memoria Press Study Guide
by Cheryl Lowe

✔ **One Year Course of 30 Weekly Lessons for Units I, II**

✔ **Daily Student Activities**

✔ **Day-by-Day, Step-by-Step Instructions**

✔ **Helpful Notes and Hints**

✔ **How to Make and Use Vocab and Grammar Cards**

✔ **What to Memorize and When**

✔ **Cumulative Grammar Test**

✔ **SPECIAL: Includes New Key for Units I & II**

Table Of Contents

Henle Latin Study Guide
© 2000 by Cheryl Lowe and Memoria Press

4103 Bishop Lane, Louisville, KY 40218
www.memoriapress.com

Preface

THE VALUE OF LATIN. Latin grammar is of immense value regardless of how far the student goes in his study. Latin trains the mind and develops study skills like no other subject. Even though you want to set high goals, you and your students are not failures if you do not finish Latin grammar or ever read Caesar, Cicero or Virgil. You can be satisfied that you have undertaken a worthy challenge and accomplished much. Your students will derive great academic benefit from the study of Latin, regardless of whether they ever read the classics or not.

TEACHING LATIN IS A REAL ART. As your skills as a teacher grow, the progress of your students will accelerate. The progress of the students in my cottage school was very slow during the first year. As my experience and confidence increased, the rate of student learning increased also. Be content with a slow pace at the beginning and lay a good foundation. Be grateful for what God has allowed you to learn and teach and do not be dissatisfied with your rate of progress. Rome was not built in a day and your knowledge of Latin won't be either.

A REALISTIC TIMETABLE. Latin grammar cannot be mastered in one year. In the 1800's Latin was begun in the middle school years and in the 1600's it was begun at the tender age of 7 or 8. In the 20th century we have reduced Latin study to the four years of high school, requiring students to learn Latin grammar in one year and then read the classical authors, Caesar, Cicero, and Virgil in grades 10-12. This has been a recipe for failure. To reinvigorate the study of Latin requires us to (1) return to a course of study that allows students several years to learn Latin grammar (2) begin Latin grammar in the early elementary years and (3) include Christian Latin for interest and accessible early reading material.

It is never too late to learn Latin. Whatever your age, there is no more valuable study than the Latin language. I began learning Latin with my elementary age children. You can learn Latin, too.

SIX YEAR SCHEDULE

If you are a homeschooler or a teacher with little experience in Latin, the following schedule is my recommendation to you for students grades 8 and up. If you accomplish more or less than this schedule but you and your students are learning Latin, working at least an hour a day, and are not stressed, then your schedule is right for you. If your students have studied in *Latina Christiana* or other Latin programs and are motivated, you can begin this schedule in the 5th or 6th grade and possibly proceed at an accelerated pace. However, Latin has a way of piling up on students and getting them discouraged. Slow down and spend time reviewing or even going back over the material a second time if your students become frustrated and discouraged.

Year 1	*Henle I* **Units 1, 2**	**pp. 1- 98**
Year 2	*Henle I* **Units 3, 4, 5**	**pp. 99 - 224**
Year 3	*Henle I* **Units 6, 7, 8**	**pp. 225 - 324**
Year 4	*Henle I* **Units 9,10,11,12**	**pp. 325 - 433**
Year 5	*Henle I* **Units 13, 14** *Henle II*	**pp. 434 - 488** **Lessons 1 - 18,** **pp. 305 – 418**
Year 6	*Henle II*	**Lessons 19 - 32,** **pp. 419 – 520** **Readings in Caesar** **and *Vulgate***

USING HENLE LATIN

1. HENLE TEXT AND GRAMMAR Most Latin books have neatly divided lessons with a similar format for every lesson. Henle does not. The lessons are of greatly varying length and the vocabulary is scattered throughout the lessons. This makes it necessary to plan each week's lesson carefully. If you follow the schedule I have suggested then you will cover about 3 pages per week. There are 103 exercises in the first year of my schedule. Again that makes about 3 ½ exercises per week. Three to four exercises per week, I think, is about right for a student without the aid of an experienced teacher. If you and your child do two exercises a week, but you understand them and they are done accurately, then that is much better than doing four exercises full of mistakes.

Most Latin books have the grammar forms in the text. Henle has the grammar forms in a *Grammar Manual* (this is the traditional way of presenting grammar). For instance turn to page 6 of the text. .... The **ASSIGNMENT** in the bottom third of the page is to memorize the declension of *terra* (Grammar, No. 31). The *Grammar Manual* has numbered sections in the left margin for each grammar topic. The number 31 is not a page number but the section number that is on page 5 of the *Grammar Manual*. Be sure to read and do each **ASSIGNMENT** in the Text by referring to the Grammar Manual.

2. CHRISTIAN CONTENT. The majority of the Christian content in Henle is in the first 100 pages. This is reassuring for students because it relates Latin to something familiar to them. A small amount of the Christian content may be incompatible with Protestant sensibilities, and will be identified in the syllabus.

3. ANSWER KEY. The answer key does not always have answers for the initial exercises which ask for the form identification. To check your answers for these exercises, look up the meaning for the grammar forms in the *Grammar Manual*.

For translation exercises it must be remembered that word order can vary and does not have to necessarily be the same as the answer key. Also some words have more than one meaning given in the vocabulary list. However, tense, voice, mood, person, number and case should not vary from the answer key. Read the short intro to the Answer Key.

4. TESTS AND QUIZZES. To save time, simplify testing. There is no need to make up tests or quizzes. Much testing can be done orally. For grammar quizzes ask students to recite or write grammar forms. For vocab quizzes, use vocab cards. For translation tests, have students copy selected sentences from their exercises for the week or month, close the book and translate.

MASTERY LEARNING

Fr. Henle teaches for mastery learning. He provides enough exercises and examples that students can actually learn and master the material rather than just be exposed to it. The information on this and the following pages will help you to teach and learn for mastery.

PERMANENT MEMORY AND TEMPORARY MEMORY. Memorized grammar forms and vocabulary are put into the temporary memory the first week. It is only through repeated drill, both oral and written, that grammar forms and vocabulary become part of the permanent memory. The goal is for the student to have *immediate* recall of memorized material. He should be able to recite grammar forms and vocabulary without hesitation and without thinking. Vocabulary and grammar forms that are mastered in this way are available for the student to draw on when he is doing translation. Translation work is difficult. If the student has to look up words and grammar, then translation work becomes pure drudgery. The reason students fail at Latin, is not because of the difficulty of the concepts, but because of the failure to master vocabulary and grammar forms.

GRAMMAR IS ABSTRACT. Latin grammar is presented both in the text and the *Grammar Manual*. The grammar explanation in the text is usually followed by vocabulary and exercises. Read the entire grammar lesson in both the text and *Grammar Manual* carefully, slowly and thoroughly. Because grammar is abstract it cannot be comprehended in just one reading. Read each grammar section more than once before attempting the exercises. If you don't understand the grammar concept, the problem may be an inadequate understanding of English grammar. Have a good English grammar nearby to consult when needed.

PRAYERS AND MUSIC. Daily recitation of prayers and singing Latin music make Latin come alive for the student. They are real Latin and they are useful and beautiful. These memorized passages develop Latin vocabulary and are useful at the appropriate time to explain grammar and syntax. *Latina Christiana* has several prayers and Latin hymns. There are five prayers in Henle and I recommend learning them. They are listed in the index under Prayers on p. 512.

NOTEBOOK. A notebook is highly recommended, loose leaf paper. The sections should be: **A.** Exercises **B.** Derivatives **C.** Grammar **D.** Notes and Word Usage **E.** Tests and Quizzes.

MASTERY LEARNING

The syllabus consists of thirty weeks. Each week is broken down into learning activities for five days. The learning activities are summarized under the five headings below. The amount of drill and review in our syllabus may not seem necessary at first, but as the vocabulary and grammar accumulate it will be a lifesaver. It is better to establish good habits at the beginning than try to catch up when you have fallen behind.

There are boxes for each daily learning activity for the student to check when the work is completed.

■ **GRAMMAR.** Read grammar lesson slowly and thoroughly, several times if necessary. Recite grammar forms orally until you can recite them from memory. Record grammar rules and forms into section **C** of notebook. In some cases you will be asked to make grammar drill cards also.

■ **VOCABULARY.** Say Latin vocabulary aloud and write words three times exactly as written in vocabulary list. Learn to spell Latin words using same techniques you use to learn English spelling. Make vocabulary cards. Record *Word Usage Notes* (underneath vocabulary list) into section **D** of notebook. Record derivatives in the **B** section of your notebook.

■ **EXERCISES.** Do about one exercise per day. If the exercise is from Latin to English, write Latin first. Check answers and correct paper. You should redo translation exercises, if necessary, until you understand them thoroughly and can do them accurately. Tests and quizzes come from the exercises. All exercises are to be written, unless otherwise indicated.

■ **DAILY FUN DRILL.** Daily oral drill of grammar forms, vocabulary and grammar cards will enable you to master the material you learn every week. The daily drill only requires about 5 minutes per day.

■ **TESTS AND QUIZZES.** Give yourself a quiz every Friday. There are three scheduled test days in the syllabus.

HOW TO MAKE AND & USE VOCABULARY CARDS

Use 3 x 5 index cards or make your own from brightly colored 8 1/2 x 11 card stock paper. You can cut it into eight equal sizes as shown to the right. Copy shops will cut the paper for you for a nominal fee.

Once you have enough blank cards, do the following:

1. Using a black or bright colored marker, write the Latin word on the front (make sure to include the genitive singular if the word is a noun)

2. Write the English translation on the back.

How to Use Vocabulary Cards

To get the full advantage from vocabulary drill, follow these steps.

1. With the Latin side of the cards up, translate from Latin to English

2. When you translate correctly from Latin to English, turn the card over (with the English side up) on the bottom of the deck. If you do not translate correctly, place the card at the bottom of the deck without turning it over (so that the Latin side is still up);

3. When you encounter a card with the English side up, translate from English to Latin. If you translate correctly, place the card aside. If you translate incorrectly, place the

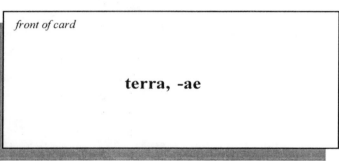

card at the bottom of the deck without turning it over (so that the English side is still up).

4. Continue this process until all of your cards are gone.

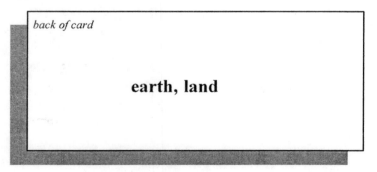

Take any cards with words that you translated correctly the first time from both Latin to English and English to Latin and place them in a separate deck to be reviewed weekly or monthly. This will keep you from needlessly reviewing words that you already know and will ensure that your daily deck of cards does not become too large.

Below you will find 35 grammar cards for the first two units of Henle. Make and use these cards in the same way as the vocabulary cards. Put the information (in the left column below) on one side, and the answer (in the right hand column below) on the other. Put the number of the card in the upper, left-hand corner.

1. Genitive singular of 1st declension nouns. — *-ae*

2. Gender of 1st decl. nouns — 1st. decl.nouns are feminine unless they name a male, like *nauta*.

3. Subject case — nominative

4. Subject/verb agreement — The verb agrees with its subject in person and number

5. Direct object case — accusative

6. Position of verb — The verb usually stands last in the sentence

7. Position of adverb — The adverb usually stands immediately before the word it modifies.

8. Case for possessives and "of" phrases — genitive

9. Genitive singular of 2nd decl. nouns — *i*

10. Gender of 2nd decl. nouns — *us*- masculine
um - neuter

11. Unique characteristic of all neuter nouns and adjectives — nominative and accusative are same, both in singular and plural.

12. Indirect object case, or the "to/for" case — dative

13. Two ways to indicate indirect objects in English — (1) "to" and (2) word order
Christ gave God glory
Christ gave glory to God

14. Prepositions take either of what two cases — ablative, accusative

15. Give the case for each preposition: *propter, post, cum, in* — acc., acc., abl., abl.

16. Predicate nominative case — nominative

17. Position of forms of *sum* — anywhere in sentence

18. Genitive singular of 3rd decl. nouns — *-is*

19. Natural gender rule — applies to ALL declensions.
A noun naming a male person is masculine (*dux*);
a noun naming a female person is feminine (*mater*).

20. Feminine endings rule for 3rd. decl. only   SOX

21. Masculine endings rule for 3rd decl. only   ERROR

22. Neuter endings rule for 3rd decl. only   LANCET

23. Appositive   A noun or a phrase that is "put beside" another noun to rename or explain it and set off by commas.

24. Agreement rule for appositives   An appositive agrees with its noun in number and case.

25. There is   *est*
    There are   *sunt*

26. Give the nominative and genitive of the 6 neuter nouns of the 3rd declension.   *flumen, fluminis*; *iter, itineris*; *corpus, coporis*; *vulnus, vulneris, agmen, agminis*; *nomen, nominis*

27. Genitive singular ending of 4th decl. nouns   *-us*

28. Gender of 4th decl. nouns   usually masculine

29. The preposition "in" with the acc. and abl.   *In* with the acc. indicates motion; *in* with ablative indicates position.

30. Genitive singular ending of 5th decl. nouns   *-ei*

31. Gender of 5th decl. nouns   usually feminine

32. The two groups of adjectives   (1) 1st/2nd declension
    (2) 3rd declension

33. Adjective/noun agreement   An adjective agrees with its noun in gender, number and case but not necessarily declension.

34. Position rule for adjectives   Adjectives of quantity usually precede their nouns, adjectives of quality usually follow.

35. Predicate adjective case   nominative

Select a pronunciation from the three that are given in the *Grammar Manual*: **(1)** the Continental system on pages 1,2 **(2)** the Roman system (Classical) on page 241, **(3)** the Italian (Christian) system on page 242. I strongly recommend the Christian pronunciation because prayers and music are your only real meaningful opportunity for oral Latin and they are always spoken in the Christian pronunciation.

Macrons - Macrons are used in to indicate the long and short vowels. It is not necessary at this stage of Latin study to require students to remember them or to reproduce them when copying Latin.

In Latin, the oral work is *not* to enable the student to learn to *speak* "authentic" Latin. The oral work is to aid the memory in retaining vocabulary and grammar forms. *Oral recitation work is extremely important in learning Latin. There is too much to learn in Latin to rely on visual memory alone.* So, it is very important to pick a simple pronunciation and recite all of your vocab and grammar forms ALOUD every day. Don't be overly concerned about whether your pronunciation is exactly right. Say Latin with confidence. Act like you know what you're doing. If you find out later you are saying some words or sounds wrong. Great! Correct yourself and go on. Remember, there are no Romans around to correct you. All nations tend to speak Latin with their own native accent anyway.

Here is a simplified system of Chrisitan Latin pronunciation to get you started:

Vowel	Pronunciation
a	"ah"
e	"ay"
i	"ee"
o	"oh"
u	"oo"

e and *i* are sometimes short, as in English "bet" and "bit."

Diphthong	Pronunciation
ae	"ay"
oe	"ay"
au	"ow"

Consonant	Pronunciation
c	"ch" before *e, i, ae, oe,* as in "church"
c	"k" before *a, o, u,* as in "cat"
gn	"gn" as in "lasagne"
j	"y" as in "yet"
s	"s" (never "z")
t	"tsee" when followed by *i* and a vowel
g	hard before *a, o, u,* as in "got"
g	soft before *e, i, ae, oe,* as in "gin"

Generally speaking, the rest of the letters are pronounced as in English.

Nouns and adjectives are studied in the first two units of Henle, pages 1-98. Some individual verbs are given so you can make sentences but verbs are not studied systematically until unit 3.

In Latin nouns are organized into 5 groups called *declensions*. Two declensions, the 2nd and the 3rd, have subgroups. You should know as you go into this study that you will be required to memorize model nouns for each of these declensions as well as the case endings. Look at the next page of this syllabus and you will see the model nouns as well as the case endings summarized to fit on a 3x5 or 4x6 card. This is what you will have to memorize and learn to use this year.

Learning declensions is not hard. I teach 3rd graders to recite these declensions and case endings in the first 10 weeks of school. They do not learn how to use every case like you will this year, but they have no trouble memorizing them and you should not either. There is only one trick to learning the declensions. Repetition. When you are introduced to a new declension, study and analyze it by comparison and contrast. Then write it out several times, both the model noun and the case endings. Say it aloud until you can say it from memory. Then write it from memory every day for two weeks and say it every day for the rest of the year.

CASE ENDINGS

Cases	Use	1st decl. F.		2nd. decl. M.		2nd. decl. N.	
		S.	*Pl.*	*S.*	*Pl.*	*S.*	*Pl.*
Nom.	*sub.*	a	ae	us	i	um	a
Gen.	*poss.*	ae	arum	i	orum	i	orum
Dat.	*I.O.*	ae	is	o	is	o	is
Acc.	*D.O.*	am	as	um	os	um	a
Abl.	*by/with/from*	a	is	o	is	o	is

3rd decl. M/F.		3rd decl. N		4th decl.		5th decl.	
S.	*Pl.*	*S.*	*Pl.*	*S.*	*Pl.*	*S.*	*Pl.*
—	es	—	a	us	us	es	es
is	i um	is	um	us	uum	ei	erum
i	ibus	i	ibus	ui	ibus	ei	ebus
em	es	—	a	um	us	em	es
e	ibus	e	ibus	u	ibus	e	ebus

MODEL NOUNS

First Declension

	feminine	
	S.	Pl.
Nominative	terra	terrae
Genitive	terrae	terrarum
Dative	terrae	terris
Accusative	terram	terras
Ablative	terra	terris

Second Declension

	masculine		*neuter*	
	S.	Pl.	S.	Pl.
Nominative	**servus**	**servi**	bellum	bella
Genitive	**servi**	**servorum**	belli	bellorum
Dative	**servo**	**servis**	bello	bellis
Accusative	**servum**	**servos**	bellum	bella
Ablative	**servo**	**servis**	bello	bellis

3rd Decl.						4th Decl.		5th Decl.	
M & F		*N*		*i stem*					
lex	leges	flumen	flumina	pars	partes	portus	portus	res	res
legis	legum	fluminis	fluminum	partis	partium	portus	portuum	rei	rerum
legi	legibus	flumini	fluminibus	parti	partibus	portui	portibus	rei	rebus
legem	leges	flumen	flumina	partem	partes	portum	portus	rem	res
lege	legibus	flumine	fluminibus	parte	partibus	portu	portibus	re	rebus

Weekly Lessons

Day 1

❏ READ: *Text, pp. 1-5.*
❏ READ AGAIN: *Text, pp. 1-5*

Day 2

You may take several weeks to memorize the meanings and uses for the cases, but the declension forms of *terra* should be committed to memory the first day.

❏ READ: *Text, pp. 6-8.* The paragraph immediately under the Assignment on p. 6, and the *Grammar* #'s 11-12, p. 2 can be omitted unless you are doing the classical pronunciation.
GRAMMAR: *Grammar, No. 31, p. 5.*
   ❏ RECITE ALOUD: Declension of *terra* 3 times. Commit to memory.
   ❏ RECORD: In grammar notebook: (1) Declension of *terra* with cases, uses and meanings;
   ❏ MAKE: Grammar Card # 1. (pp. 9-10)
VOCABULARY: *Text, p. 7*
   ❏ SAY: Vocabulary words aloud three times.
   ❏ WRITE: Vocabulary words three times.
   ❏ MAKE: Vocabulary cards.
❏ EXERCISES: *Exercise 1, p. 8*, orally and written.

At the end of Day 2 you should be able to recite and write the 1st Decl. from memory.

Day 3

You may do exercises 2 and 3 orally. Be sure to say the Latin words aloud before you translate.

❏ READ AGAIN: *Text, p. 6.*
❏ EXERCISE: *Exercises 2,3 pp. 8-9.*
❏ CHECK: All answers.

While it is not necessary to remember all of the long and short vowel markings, please note that the ablative singular is distinguished from the nominative singular by the macron.

Day 4

❏ READ: *Text, Lesson 1, Section 2, p. 9*
❏ EXERCISE: *Exercise 4, p. 9*
❏ CHECK: All answers.
❏ MAKE: Grammar Card # 2
❏ RECORD: Derivatives (Related English Words, p. 7) in section **B** of Latin notebook. Add these derivatives: *terrestrial, territory, Nautilis, victorious, Pennsylvania, Transylvania, glorious.*

You may do exercise 4 orally

Day 5

❏ WEEKLY QUIZ—Recite and write declension of *terra* from memory. Quiz with vocab cards, making sure you can spell all words correctly.

Exercises 5-7
pp. 9-15

LESSON 2

Day 1

Except for diagramming, you may do Ex. 5 and 6 orally, but read orally in both Latin and English

❏ READ: *Text, Lesson 1, No.3, pp. 9-11.*
❏ MAKE GRAMMAR CARDS # 3, 4
VOCABULARY: *Text, p. 11*
    ❏ SAY: Vocabulary words aloud three times.
    ❏ WRITE: Vocabulary words three times.
    ❏ MAKE: Vocabulary cards.
❏ EXERCISES: *Exercise 5, p. 11.*
❏ CHECK: All your answers. ❏ REDO: Incorrect answers.

Day 2

The picture and info on pages 12, 13 are somewhat outdated since the Catholic Church has gone to the vernacular in its liturgy. The Latin Mass is still permitted, however, and there may be one in your area if you would like to hear one.

❏ READ AGAIN: *Lesson 1, No.3*
❏ READ: *Reading No. 1, p. 13, No. 4, pp 13-14.*
❏ MAKE GRAMMAR CARDS # 5, 6
❏ VOCABULARY: *Text, p. 14*
    ❏ SAY: Vocabulary words aloud three times.
    ❏ WRITE: Vocabulary words three times.
    ❏ MAKE: Vocabulary cards.
❏ EXERCISES: *Exercise 6, p. 14.*
❏ CHECK and ❏ REDO: Incorrect answers

Day 3

Translating from English to Latin takes much more time than the reverse. Schedule plenty of time and do exercises over if necessary until you get all of the endings correct. Do this exercise written.

❏ READ: *Text, p. 15, "Talking Latin No. 1"*
❏ MAKE GRAMMAR CARD # 7
❏ EXERCISES: *Exercise 7 (1-5) , p. 15, written.*
❏ CHECK and ❏ REDO: Incorrect answers

Day 4

❏ DECLINE: *provincia* in the vocabulary on p. 14
❏ EXERCISES: *Exercise 7 (6-11) , p. 15, written.*
❏ WRITE: Names of cases three times. Commit to memory.
❏ RECORD: Derivatives (Related English Words, pp. 11 and 14) in derivative section of Latin notebook. Add *oral* and *video*.

Day 5

❏ WEEKLY QUIZ—Copy No. 3 from exercises 5-7, close book and translate. Quiz with vocab cards, making sure you can spell all words correctly.

LESS ON 3   **Exercises 8-11**
pp. 16-18

❏ READ: *Lesson 1, No. 5, p. 16*
❏ MAKE GRAMMAR CARD # 8
❏ EXERCISES: *Exercise 8, p. 16*
❏ CHECK: All answers. ❏ REDO: Incorrect answers
❏ DAILY FUN DRILL

Day 1
You may do exercises 8 and 9 orally,
but read aloud in both Latin and English

❏ READ AGAIN: *Lesson 1, No. 5, p. 16*
❏ EXERCISE: *Exercise 9, p. 16*
❏ CHECK: All answers. ❏ REDO: Answers you missed in the exercise
❏ DAILY FUN DRILL

Day 2

❏ READ: *Lesson 2, The Second Declension, p. 17*
GRAMMAR:
    ❏ RECORD: Declension of *servus* (*Grammar*, No. 34) in section **C** of your Latin notebook
    ❏ RECITE ALOUD: Declension of *servus* three times. Contrast and compare to 1st declension. Commit to memory.
    ❏ MAKE GRAMMAR CARDS # 9, 10
VOCABULARY: *Text, p. 17*
    ❏ SAY: Vocabulary words aloud three times.
    ❏ WRITE: Vocabulary words three times.
    ❏ MAKE: Vocabulary cards.
❏ EXERCISES: *Exercise 10, p. 18, oral and written.*
❏ CHECK: All your answers. ❏ REDO: Any answers you missed in the exercise
❏ DAILY FUN DRILL

Day 3

❏ READ AGAIN: *Lesson 2, p. 17*
❏ EXERCISES: *Exercise 11 (1-15), p. 18*
❏ RECORD: Derivatives (in "Related English Words," p. 17) in derivative section of Latin notebook. Add *deity* and *video.*
❏ DAILY FUN DRILL

Day 4

You may do exercises 11 and 12 orally, but read aloud in both Latin and English

❏ WEEKLY QUIZ

Day 5

DAILY FUN DRILL:
    ❏ RECITE: *Pater Noster*, pp. 388-389
    ❏ RECITE: All grammar forms: *terra, servus,* and case endings
    ❏ DRILL: Vocabulary cards, grammar cards.

The Second Declension (continued)

LESSON 4

Day 1
- ❏ REREAD: *Lesson 2, p. 17*
- ❏ EXERCISES: *Exercise 11 (16-30), p. 19; Exercise 12, p. 19*
- ❏ CHECK: answers and ❏ REDO: Incorrect answers
- ❏ DAILY FUN DRILL

Day 2

For all exercises requiring translation of Latin sentences (such as 13, 17, 19, etc.) follow this procedure (1)read complete sentence orally in Latin, (2)copy Latin sentence (3)write out translation in English.

- ❏ EXERCISES: *Exercise 13, p. 19*
- ❏ CHECK: All answers ❏ REDO: Incorrect answers.
- ❏ DAILY FUN DRILL

Day 3

Redo any exercise in which you make more than one mistake. Remember all exercises are to be done written unless otherwise indicated.

- ❏ EXERCISES: *Exercise 14 (1-6), p. 20*
- ❏ CHECK: All your answers. ❏ REDO: Incorrect answers
- ❏ DAILY FUN DRILL

Day 4

Be accurate and thorough in your translation work. **Accuracy, not speed is your goal.**

- ❏ EXERCISES: *Exercise 14 (7-11), p. 20*
- ❏ CHECK: All your answers. ❏ REDO: Incorrect answers
- ❏ DAILY FUN DRILL

Day 5
- ❏ WEEKLY QUIZ

Extra Credit
- ❏ Translate boxed saying on p. 20. Give the case and number for the forms of *servus*.

DAILY FUN DRILL:
- ❏ RECITE: *Pater Noster*, pp. 388-389
- ❏ RECITE: All grammar forms: *terra, servus,* and case endings
- ❏ DRILL: Vocabulary cards, grammar cards.

The second declension has two groups of nouns: masculine and neuter. In the plural, neuter nouns end in *a* in the nominative and accusative. In the first declension, nouns end in *a* in the nominative and ablative. This will give you trouble at first.

❏ READ: *Unit 1, Lesson 2, No. 2, p. 20*
GRAMMAR:
    ❏ RECITE ALOUD: *Grammar, No. 37, p. 7*: Declension of *bellum* three times. Compare and contrast to previous declensions. Commit to memory.
    ❏ MAKE GRAMMAR CARD # 11
    ❏ RECORD: In section **C** of Latin notebook: Declension of *bellum*
VOCABULARY: *Text, p. 21*
    ❏ SAY: Vocabulary words aloud three times.
    ❏ WRITE: Vocabulary words three times.
    ❏ MAKE: Vocabulary cards.
❏ EXERCISES: *Exercise 15, p. 21*
❏ CHECK: All your answers. ❏ REDO: Incorrect answers.
❏ DAILY FUN DRILL

Day 1

You may do exercises 15 and 16 orally, Latin first, then English.

❏ READ AGAIN: *Unit 1, Lesson 2, No. 2, p. 20*
❏ EXERCISES: *Exercise 16, p. 21*
❏ CHECK: All your answers. ❏ REDO: Incorrect answers.
❏ DAILY FUN DRILL

Day 2

❏ READ: *Note at bottom of p. 21.* Record in section **D** of notebook.
❏ EXERCISES: *Exercise 17, p. 22.*
❏ CHECK: All your answers. ❏ REDO: Incorrect answers.
❏ DAILY FUN DRILL

Day 3 Remember the procedure. (1) read complete sentence orally in Latin, (2) copy Latin sentence (3) write out translation in English.

❏ EXERCISES: *Exercise 18, p. 22* (omit # 2)
❏ CHECK: All your answers. ❏ REDO: Incorrect answers.
❏ RECORD: Derivatives (in "Related English Words," p. 21) in derivative section of Latin notebook. Add *celestial, bellicose, peril,* and *perilous.*
❏ DECLINE: All nouns in vocabulary, p. 21.
❏ DAILY FUN DRILL

Day 4

❏ WEEKLY QUIZ

Day 5

DAILY FUN DRILL:
    ❏ RECITE: *Pater Noster*, pp. 388-389
    ❏ RECITE: All grammar forms: *terra, servus, bellum,* and case endings
    ❏ DRILL: Vocabulary cards, grammar cards.

LESSON 6

Giving and *telling* verbs often have indirect objects. In this text whenever you see the Latin verb for **give**, be sure and look for an indirect object in the dative case. The dative case is often called the *to or for case.*

We have two ways of indicating a direct object in English: by using the preposition "to" or by placing the indirect object before the direct object in the sentence. In Latin there is only one way to indicate an indirect object: by putting it in the dative case. The indirect object in Latin may precede or follow the direct object.

Day 1

If you are having difficulties in translating from *Latin to English*, **find the subject and verb first,** then a direct object if there is one. The rest of the sentence will start to fall into place. If you cannot find a subject use the pronoun in the verb.

❏ READ: *Lesson 2, No. 3, p. 22, 23*
❏ MAKE GRAMMAR CARD # 12, 13
VOCABULARY: *Text, p. 23*
   ❏ SAY: Vocabulary words aloud three times.
   ❏ WRITE: Vocabulary words three times.
   ❏ MAKE: Vocabulary cards.
❏ EXERCISES: *Exercise 19, p. 23.* For ex. 19, do in this order: 1,3,5,7,4, 8, 6, 10, and be careful with 9, 11, 2
❏ CHECK: All your answers. ❏ REDO: Incorrect answers.
❏ DAILY FUN DRILL

Day 2

If you are making many errors in *English to Latin* translation you should **diagram** the English sentences first. Diagramming will help you to slow down, analyze what you are trying to translate and improve **Day 3** the accuracy of your work.

❏ READ AGAIN: *Lesson 2, No. 3, p. 22, 23*
❏ EXERCISES: *Exercise 20, sentences 1-4, pp. 23-24*
❏ CHECK: All your answers. ❏ REDO: Incorrect answers.
❏ DAILY FUN DRILL

❏ EXERCISES: *Exercise 20, sentences, 5-8, pp. 23-24*
❏ CHECK: All your answers. ❏ REDO: Incorrect answers.
❏ DAILY FUN DRILL
❏ DECLINE: *gladius.*

Day 4

❏ EXERCISES: *Exercise 21, p. 24.*
❏ CHECK: All your answers. ❏ REDO: Incorrect answers.
❏ RECORD: Derivatives (Related English Words, p. 23) in derivative section of Latin notebook. Add *dedicate.*
❏ DAILY FUN DRILL

Day 5

❏ WEEKLY QUIZ

DAILY FUN DRILL:
   ❏ RECITE: *Pater Noster*, pp. 388-389
   ❏ RECITE: All grammar forms: *terra, servus, bellum,* and case endings
   ❏ DRILL: Vocabulary cards, grammar cards.

Be sure to learn the case each preposition takes. The two prepositions starting with **p** take the accusative, the other two take the ablative. The ablative is often called the *by, with or from case.*

❑ READ: *Lesson 2, No. 4, p. 24.*
❑ MAKE GRAMMAR CARDS # 14, 15
VOCABULARY: *Text, p. 25.*
   ❑ SAY: Vocabulary words aloud three times.
   ❑ WRITE: Vocabulary words three times.
   ❑ MAKE: Vocabulary cards.
❑ EXERCISE: *Exercise 22 (1-20) p. 25.*
❑ CHECK: All your answers. ❑ REDO: Incorrect answers.
❑ DAILY FUN DRILL

Day 1

You may do exercise 22 orally, first in Latin then in English.

❑ READ AGAIN: *Lesson 2, No. 4*
❑ EXERCISE: *Exercise 22 (21-40), p. 26.*
❑ CHECK: All your answers. ❑ REDO: Incorrect answers.
❑ DAILY FUN DRILL

Day 2

❑ EXERCISE: *Exercise 23 (1-13), p. 26-27.*
❑ CHECK: All your answers. ❑ REDO: Incorrect answers.
❑ DECLINE: All nouns in vocabulary, p. 25.
❑ DAILY FUN DRILL

Day 3

❑ EXERCISE: *Exercise 23 (14-25), p. 27.*
❑ CHECK: All your answers. ❑ REDO: Incorrect answers.
❑ RECORD: Derivatives (Related English Words, p. 25) in derivative section of Latin notebook.
❑ DAILY FUN DRILL

Day 4

Remember, all exercises should be written unless indicated otherwise.

❑ WEEKLY QUIZ

Day 5

DAILY FUN DRILL:
   ❑ RECITE: *Pater Noster*, pp. 388-389
   ❑ RECITE: All grammar forms: *terra, servus, bellum,* and case endings
   ❑ DRILL: Vocabulary cards, grammar cards

This is a summary of the cases and their uses (in random order) to use for drill. Be sure you know it thoroughly.

Use	Case
Subject	nominative
Predicate nominative	nominative
to/for	dative
possessive	genitive
indirect object	dative
"of" case	genitive
predicate adjective	nominative
by/with/from case	ablative
prepositional objects	ablative, accusative
direct object	accusative

PRONUNCIATION RULES

The Alphabet

The Latin alphabet has no "w". Words with "y" are of Greek origin.

Vowels

In Christian Latin vowels are usually long.

Vowel	Long	Example
a	'father' (ah)	ad, mater
e	'they' (ay)	me, video
i	'machine' (ee)	video, qui
o	'no' (oh)	porta, omnis
u	'rule' (oo)	cum, sumus

Sometimes the vowels **e** and **i** tend toward the short vowel sounds of English.

Diphthongs

Diphthongs are two vowels together that are pronounced as one continuous sound.

Dipthong	Pronunciation	Example
ae }	like *e* in 'they' (ay)	saepe, praemium, proelium
oe }		
au	like ou in out (ow)	laudo, nauta

Consonants

Most of the consonants are pronounced as in English, with the following exceptions.

Consonant	Pronunciation	Examples
c	before *e, i, ae, oe* like *ch* in 'charity'	decem, cibus, caelum
c	before other letters, hard *c* as in 'cut'	clamo, culpa
gn	like *gn* as in 'lasagne'	pugno, regnum
j	like *y* as in 'yet'	judico, Jesus
s	like *s* as in 'sing' (never like *z*)	tres, mensa
t	when followed by *i* and a vowel, like *tsee*	gratia, tertius nuntius

In words of three or more syllables. the accent mark indicates the stressed syllable. It is not necessary for the student to learn the location of the accent mark, or to copy it when writing Latin.

These are long exercises. Redo them if necessary and try to get every ending correct, especially on the English to Latin in Ex. 25. In both exercises, underline the predicate nominative in English and Latin.

❏ READ: *Lesson 2, No. 5, pp. 27-28*   **Day 1**
GRAMMAR:
   ❏ MAKE GRAMMAR CARDS # 16, 17
   ❏ RECITE ALOUD: Conjugation of *sum* three times. Commit to memory
❏ EXERCISE: *Exercise 24 (1-13), p. 28*
❏ CHECK: All your answers. ❏ REDO: Incorrect answers.
❏ DAILY FUN DRILL

❏ READ AGAIN: *Lesson 2, No. 5, pp. 27-28*   **Day 2**
❏ EXERCISE: *Exercise 24 (14-25), p. 28*
❏ CHECK: All your answers. ❏ REDO: Incorrect answers.
❏ DAILY FUN DRILL

❏ EXERCISE: *Exercise 25 (1-9), p. 29*   **Day 3**
❏ CHECK: All your answers. ❏ REDO: Incorrect answers.
❏ DAILY FUN DRILL

❏ EXERCISE: *Exercise 25, nos. 10-17, p. 29.*   **Day 4**
❏ CHECK: All your answers. ❏ REDO: Incorrect answers.
❏ READ: *"Talking Latin No. 2" p. 29.*
❏ DAILY FUN DRILL

❏ WEEKLY QUIZ   **Day 5**

DAILY FUN DRILL:
   ❏ RECITE: *Pater Noster,* pp. 388-389
   ❏ RECITE: All grammar forms: declensions of *terra, servus, bellum,* case endings and conjugation of *sum.*
   ❏ DRILL: Vocabulary cards, grammar cards

Exercises 26-27
pp. 30-34

LESSON 9

This is a short assignment. Review all previous work and then take practice tests and a real test on Friday. Next week you will begin the third declension. You cannot learn the third declension until you can recite the first and second declensions from memory without even thinking. They should be part of your permanent memory.

Day 1

❏ READ: *Lesson 2, No. 6, p. 31.*
❏ RECORD: Vocabulary Note, p. 31, in section **D** of your Latin notebook.
VOCABULARY: *Text, p. 31.*
   ❏ SAY: Vocabulary words aloud three times.
   ❏ WRITE: Vocabulary words three times.
   ❏ MAKE: Vocabulary cards.
❏ EXERCISE: *Exercise 26, p. 31*
❏ CHECK: All your answers. ❏ REDO: Incorrect answers.
❏ DAILY FUN DRILL

Day 2

For your practice test 1 select the first # of each exercise. Copy, close book and translate. Repeat for additional practice tests and real test, selecting different #'s each time.

❏ READ AGAIN: *Lesson 2, No. 6*
❏ EXERCISE: *Exercise 27, p. 33* (non-Catholics may omit this exercise)
❏ CHECK: All your answers. ❏ REDO: Incorrect answers.
❏ DAILY FUN DRILL
❏ PRACTICE TEST 1

Day 3

❏ READ: "Reading No. 2," p. 33, 34
❏ DAILY FUN DRILL
❏ PRACTICE TEST 2

Day 4

❏ DAILY FUN DRILL
❏ PRACTICE TEST 3

Day 5

❏ TAKE REVIEW TEST

DAILY FUN DRILL:
   ❏ RECITE: *Pater Noster,* pp. 388-389
   ❏ RECITE: All grammar forms: declensions of *terra, servus, bellum,* case endings and conjugation of *sum.*
   ❏ DRILL: Vocabulary cards, grammar cards

The first two declensions are a unit because they contain all three genders. The third declension is another unit because it also contains all three genders. The Third declension is more difficult than the first two declensions for two reasons. (1) The gender of each noun has to be learned individually because there are no characteristic endings for the three genders as there are in the first two declensions (a-F, us- M, um-N). (2) Third declension nouns usually change spelling from the nominative to the genitive. The nouns are just more difficult words.

❑ READ: *Lesson 3, p. 35, also No. 1, p. 35. Grammar, Nos. 45-51, p. 9*
❑ MAKE GRAMMAR CARDS# 18-22
❑ EXERCISE: *Exercise 30 (#1 only), p. 37.* ❑ CHECK ❑ REDO
❑ DAILY FUN DRILL

Day 1
Omit # 52 in Grammar, p. 9. Instead just remember that there are some exceptions to the SOX, ERROR and LANCET rules.

❑ REREAD: *Lesson 3, p. 35, also No. 1, p. 35. Grammar, Nos. 45-51, p. 9*
❑ READ: *Lesson 3, No. 3, p. 36. (Skip No. 2 and ex. 28, 29)*
GRAMMAR: *Grammar, No. 57, p. 10*
    ❑ RECITE ALOUD: Declension of *lex* three times. Commit to memory.
    ❑ RECORD: In section **C** of Latin notebook: Declension of *lex*
VOCABULARY: *Text, p. 36.*
    ❑ SAY: Vocabulary words aloud three times.
    ❑ WRITE: Vocabulary words three times.
    ❑ MAKE: Vocabulary cards.
❑ DECLINE: All nouns in vocabulary, but decline veritas and lux in singular only
❑ EXERCISE: *Exercise 31, p. 37.* ❑ CHECK ❑ REDO

Day 2
Remember "g" is soft before e and i and hard before u, o, a.

Be sure to read the note at the bottom of page 35. Nouns that are exceptions to SOX, ERROR and LANCET will have their gender indicated by a small *f, m,*or *n* in the vocabulary list.

Exercises 31, 32 may be done orally.

❑ EXERCISE: *Exercise 32-33, p. 37; Ex. 34 (1-6)* ❑ CHECK ❑ REDO
❑ DAILY FUN DRILL

Day 3

❑ EXERCISE: *Exercise 34 (7-12); Ex. 35 (1-3).* ❑ CHECK ❑ REDO
❑ RECORD: Derivatives (Related English Words), p. 36 in Latin notebook.
❑ DAILY FUN DRILL

Day 4

❑ EXERCISE: *Exercise 35 (4-6), p. 38.* ❑ CHECK ❑ REDO
❑ WEEKLY QUIZ

Day 5

DAILY FUN DRILL:
    ❑ RECITE: *Pater Noster*, pp. 388-389, *Gloria Patri*, p. 118
    ❑ RECITE: All grammar forms: declensions of *terra, servus, bellum, lex,* case endings and conjugation of *sum.*
    ❑ DRILL: Vocabulary cards, grammar cards

LESSON 11

An appositive renames its noun like a predicate nominative, but it is not linked to the noun by a linking verb; it is in apposition to it - positioned directly next to its noun. An appositive must agree with its noun in number and case--*and its noun can be in any case!* In English the appositive is set off by commas but in Latin an appositive may precede or follows its noun without commas. The appositive may be made up of more than one word, such as "Filius Dei". In such cases the additional words are in a case determined by their own function.

Day 1

Underline the noun and its appositive in both English and Latin and identify the case. Which sentence does not have an appositive?

❏ READ: *Unit 1, Lesson 3, No. 4, pp. 38-39*
❏ MAKE GRAMMAR CARDS # 23, 24
VOCABULARY: *Text, p. 39.*
   ❏ SAY: Vocabulary words aloud three times.
   ❏ WRITE: Vocabulary words three times.
   ❏ MAKE: Vocabulary cards.
❏ EXERCISE: *Exercise 36, p. 40. Do this exercise in this order: 3, 4, 5, 6, 7, 8, 1, 2.* (In sentence # 2 the appositive is not set off with commas)
❏ CHECK: All your answers. ❏ REDO: Incorrect answers.
❏ DAILY FUN DRILL

Day 2

Underline the noun and its appositive. Identify the case of the noun and you will know what case to put the appositive in.

❏ READ AGAIN: *Unit 1, Lesson 3, No. 4, p. 38-39*
❏ EXERCISE: *Exercise 37, p. 40.*
❏ CHECK: All your answers. ❏ REDO: Incorrect answers.
❏ DAILY FUN DRILL

Day 3

❏ READ AGAIN: *Unit 1, Lesson 3, No. 4*
❏ EXERCISE: *Exercise 38 (1-4), p. 41.*
❏ CHECK: All your answers. ❏ REDO: Incorrect answers.
❏ DAILY FUN DRILL

Day 4

❏ EXERCISE: *Exercise 38 (5-7), Ex. 39*
❏ CHECK: All your answers. ❏ REDO: Incorrect answers.
❏ RECORD: Derivatives (Related English Words), p. 39.
❏ DAILY FUN DRILL

Day 5

❏ WEEKLY QUIZ

DAILY FUN DRILL:
   ❏ RECITE: *Pater Noster*, pp. 388-389, *Gloria Patri*, p. 118
   ❏ RECITE: All grammar forms: declensions of *terra, servus, bellum, lex,* case endings and conjugation of *sum.*
   ❏ DRILL: Vocabulary cards, grammar cards

Extra Credit

❏ Translate boxed saying on p. 40 and find the chapter and verse in the Bible from which it comes. Give the case of these nouns and tell whether they are predicate nominatives or appositives: Christi, servus, via, veritas, vita.

❏ EXERCISE: *Exercise 40, p. 42.*
❏ CHECK: All your answers. ❏ REDO: Incorrect answers.
❏ DAILY FUN DRILL

❏ READ: *Lesson 3, No. 5, p. 42.*
❏ MAKE GRAMMAR CARD # 25
VOCABULARY: *Text, p. 42.*
    ❏ SAY: Vocabulary words aloud three times.
    ❏ WRITE: Vocabulary words three times.
    ❏ MAKE: Vocabulary cards.
    ❏ ANSWER: Questions # 2, under Note, p. 43.
    ❏ DECLINE: All nouns in vocabulary.
    ❏ RECORD: Note, p. 43, #2 in section **D** of Latin notebook.
❏ EXERCISE: *Exercise 41, p. 43*
❏ CHECK: All your answers. ❏ REDO: Incorrect answers.
❏ DAILY FUN DRILL

❏ READ AGAIN: *Lesson 3, No. 5, p. 42.*
❏ EXERCISE: *Exercise 42 (1-5), p. 43*
❏ CHECK: All your answers. ❏ REDO: Incorrect answers.
❏ DAILY FUN DRILL

❏ READ: *"Talking Latin No. 3," p. 44*
❏ RECORD: Derivatives in "Related English Words," p. 43 in Latin notebook.
❏ EXERCISE: *Exercise 42(6-9), pp. 43-44*
❏ CHECK: All your answers. ❏ REDO: Incorrect answers.
❏ DAILY FUN DRILL

❏ WEEKLY QUIZ

DAILY FUN DRILL:
    ❏ RECITE: *Pater Noster*, pp. 388-389, *Gloria Patri*, p. 118
    ❏ RECITE: All grammar forms: declensions of *terra, servus, bellum, lex,*
    case endings and conjugation of *sum.*
    ❏ DRILL: Vocabulary cards, grammar cards

❏ Translate boxed saying on p. 43. Explain the case of each of the nouns in the saying.

Day 1 Why do you think the 3rd declension has *um* for the genitive plural ending instead of *orum*? What would *imperator* be in the genitive plural if it had the *orum* ending as the first two declensions do?

Day 2

Day 3
Go back through your vocabulary cards and add the gender (*m, f, n*) of the nouns. Include gender in your vocab drill from now on.

Day 4

Day 5

Extra Credit

The declension of *pars*

Exercises 43-47
pp. 44-46

LESSON 13

On the declension chart on p. 13, there is not a separate set of case endings for -**i** stems, but there is a bold -**i** in the genitive plural of the regular case endings for the 3rd declension.

There are some nouns in the 3rd declension that are called **i stems.** They are declined just like *lex* except that they have an **i** in the genitive plural. The declension of **i stems** is given in # 58 (pars) on p. 10 of the *Grammar Manual.* The rules for identifying **i stems** are given in Nos. 59-63 on p. 10 of the *Grammar Manual.* You may learn these if you want to. For now, however, I recommend just remembering that there are a few nouns in this text which are **i-stems,** five of which are in this lesson. **I-stems** are just a little irregularity in the 3rd declension.

Day 1

Which word in today's vocab has the same ending in the nominative S. and Pl.?

❏ READ: *Lesson 3, No. 6, pp. 44-45.*
GRAMMAR:
    ❏ SAY ALOUD: The declension of pars three times.
    ❏ RECORD: Declension of *pars, Grammar,* No. 58. Commit to memory
VOCABULARY: *Text,* p. 44.
    ❏ SAY: Vocabulary words aloud three times.
    ❏ WRITE: Vocabulary words three times.
    ❏ MAKE: Vocabulary cards. Be sure to add gender to your vocab cards.
    ❏ RECORD: Vocabulary Note, p 45 in section **D** of your Latin notebook.

You may do Ex. 44 orally

❏ EXERCISE: *Exercise 43 and 44, p. 45*
❏ CHECK: All your answers. ❏ REDO: Incorrect answers.
❏ DAILY FUN DRILL

Day 2

❏ EXERCISE: *Exercise 45, p. 46*
❏ CHECK: All your answers. ❏ REDO: Incorrect answers.
❏ DECLINE: collis, caedes
❏ DAILY FUN DRILL

Day 3

❏ EXERCISE: *Exercise 46, p. 46*
❏ CHECK: All your answers. ❏ REDO: Incorrect answers.
❏ DAILY FUN DRILL

Day 4

❏ EXERCISE: *Exercise 47, p. 46*
❏ CHECK: All your answers. ❏ REDO: Incorrect answers.
❏ RECORD: Derivatives in "Related English Words," p. 45.
❏ DAILY FUN DRILL

Day 5

❏ WEEKLY QUIZ

DAILY FUN DRILL:
    ❏ RECITE: *Pater Noster*, pp. 388-389, *Gloria Patri,* p. 118
    ❏ RECITE: All grammar forms: declensions of *terra, servus, bellum, lex, pars,* case endings and conjugation of *sum*
    ❏ DRILL: Vocabulary cards, grammar cards.

Extra Credit

❏ Translate boxed saying on p. 45. Explain the case of each of the nouns in the saying.

HENLE LATIN STUDY GUIDE

This is a review week. There is no new grammar.

VOCABULARY: *Text, p. 47*   **Day 1**
   ❏ SAY: Vocabulary words aloud three times.
   ❏ WRITE: Vocabulary words three times.
   ❏ MAKE: Vocabulary cards. Remember to add gender to your vocab. cards and   The gen. pl. is given for
   to indicate i-stem nouns.   *frater, pater, mater* to
❏ DECLINE: All nouns in vocabulary, p. 47   show that they are
❏ EXERCISES: *Exercise 48, Ex. 49 (no. 1 only)*   not **i-stems**. Mons is an
❏ CHECK: All your answers. ❏ REDO: Incorrect answers.   **i-stem.**
❏ DAILY FUN DRILL

❏ EXERCISES: *Exercises 50, 51 (translate only)*   **Day 2**
❏ CHECK: All your answers. ❏ REDO: Incorrect answers.
❏ DAILY FUN DRILL

❏ EXERCISES: *Exercise 52* Non-Catholics may omit Ex 52.5.   **Day 3**
❏ CHECK: All your answers. ❏ REDO: Incorrect answers.
❏ DAILY FUN DRILL

❏ READ: *Note On Reading Latin, pp. 48-49*   **Day 4**
❏ EXERCISES: *Exercise 53.*
❏ CHECK: All your answers. ❏ REDO: Incorrect answers.
❏ RECORD: Derivatives (Related English Words, p. 47) in derivative section of
Latin notebook. Add *fraternity, mount, clamor, principality*
❏ DAILY FUN DRILL

❏ WEEKLY QUIZ   **Day 5**

DAILY FUN DRILL:
   ❏ RECITE: *Pater Noster*, pp. 388-389; *Gloria Patri*, p. 118
   ❏ RECITE: All grammar forms: *terra, servus, bellum, lex, pars,* case
   endings, and the conjugation of *sum*
   ❏ DRILL: Vocabulary cards, grammar cards.

Exercises 54-57
pp. 51-53

LESSON 15

These 3rd declension neuter nouns are difficult. The vowel changes from the nominative to the genitive must be written and pronounced orally until they are mastered. Do not be discouraged. The next two declensions are easy. The third declension is the hardest and this is the end of it. You have three model nouns for the 3rd declension: *lex, pars, and flumen.* Recite them daily and you will master them in no time.

Day 1

Three of these nouns do not follow the LANCET rule. The best policy is just to remember that there are 6 neuter nouns in this first section of the book, put them on one drill card and memorize them.

You may do Ex. 54 orally.

❏ READ: *Lesson 3, No. 8, p. 51.*
VOCABULARY: *Text, p. 51*
   ❏ SAY: Vocabulary words aloud three times.
   ❏ WRITE: Vocabulary words three times.
   ❏ MAKE: Vocabulary cards.
GRAMMAR: *Grammar, p. 11, No. 64*
   ❏ SAY: Declension of flumen aloud three times. Commit to memory
   ❏ RECORD: Declension of flumen in Latin notebook
   ❏ DECLINE: All nouns in vocabulary, p. 51, orally and on paper.
   ❏ MAKE GRAMMAR CARD # 26
❏ EXERCISES: *Exercise 54, pp. 51-52*
❏ CHECK: All your answers. ❏ REDO: Incorrect answers.
❏ DAILY FUN DRILL

Day 2

❏ READ AGAIN: *Lesson 3, No. 8, p. 51.*
❏ EXERCISES: *Exercise 55, p. 52.*
❏ CHECK: All your answers. ❏ REDO: Incorrect answers.
❏ DAILY FUN DRILL

Day 3

❏ EXERCISES: *Exercise 56, p. 52*
❏ CHECK: All your answers. ❏ REDO: Incorrect answers.
❏ DAILY FUN DRILL

Day 4

❏ EXERCISES: *Exercise 57, p. 52-53.*
❏ CHECK: All your answers. ❏ REDO: Incorrect answers.
❏ DAILY FUN DRILL
❏ RECORD: Derivatives (Related English Words, p. 51) in derivative section of Latin notebook. Add *itinerary, corpse, vulnerable, invulnerable, fluid*
❏ DAILY FUN DRILL

Day 5

❏ WEEKLY QUIZ

DAILY FUN DRILL:
   ❏ RECITE: *Pater Noster*, pp. 388-389; *Gloria Patri*, p. 118
   ❏ RECITE: All grammar forms: *terra, servus, bellum, lex, pars, flumen,* case endings and the conjugation of *sum*
   ❏ DRILL: Vocabulary cards, grammar cards.

There is no new grammar in this lesson, just a review of the 3rd declension. Work hard and do all of your exercises, more than once if necessary, until you understand them thoroughly and can do them without errors.

❏ READ: *Text, Lesson 3, No. 9, p. 53*   **Day 1**
VOCABULARY: *Text, p. 53*
     ❏ SAY: Vocabulary words aloud three times.
     ❏ WRITE: Vocabulary words three times.
     ❏ MAKE: Vocabulary cards.
     ❏ RECORD: Note under vocabulary into Word Usage section of your note-
     book.
❏ EXERCISE: *Exercise 58*
❏ CHECK: All your answers. ❏ REDO: Incorrect answers.
❏ DAILY FUN DRILL

You may do Ex. 58 **orally.** This is a good drill exercise to do several times.

❏ EXERCISE: *Exercise 59 (1-10)*   **Day 2**
❏ CHECK: All your answers. ❏ REDO: Incorrect answers.
❏ DAILY FUN DRILL

❏ EXERCISE: *Exercise 59 (11-15), Ex. 61*   **Day 3**
❏ CHECK: All your answers. ❏ REDO: Incorrect answers.
❏ DAILY FUN DRILL

❏ EXERCISE: *Exercise 60 (1-5)*   **Day 4**
❏ CHECK: All your answers. ❏ REDO: Incorrect answers.
❏ DAILY FUN DRILL
❏ RECORD: Derivatives (Related English Words, p. 53)

❏ WEEKLY QUIZ   **Day 5**

DAILY FUN DRILL:
     ❏ RECITE: *Pater Noster*, pp. 388-389; *Gloria Patri*, p. 118
     ❏ RECITE: All grammar forms: *terra, servus, bellum, lex, pars, flumen,*
     case endings and the conjugation of *sum*
     ❏ DRILL: Vocabulary cards, grammar cards

The Fourth declension, thankfully, has only one model to learn. The fourth and fifth declensions are small declensions. They have few words.   If you are doing the Christian pronunciation you probably have not paid much attention to the macrons over the long vowels.   In the 4th declension the gen. S., and nom. and acc. Pl. have the macrons over the vowel, while the nom. S. does not.   You may want to keep this in mind in doing your exercises in this section.

Day 1

❏ READ: *Lesson 4, No. 1, p. 56; Note under vocabulary, p. 56*
VOCABULARY: *Text, p. 56*
    ❏ SAY: Vocabulary words aloud three times.
    ❏ WRITE: Vocabulary words three times.
    ❏ MAKE: Vocabulary cards.
GRAMMAR: *Grammar, p. 12, No. 65*
    ❏ SAY: Declension of *portus* aloud, three times. Commit to memory
    ❏ RECORD: Declension of *portus*, *Grammar 65* in Latin notebook.
    ❏ MAKE GRAMMAR CARDS # 27, 28
❏ EXERCISES: *Exercise 62, p. 57., Ex. 60 (5-10)*
❏ CHECK: All your answers. ❏ REDO: Incorrect answers.
❏ DAILY FUN DRILL

Do not confuse
porta, ae,   gate,
portus, us   harbor

Day 2

❏ EXERCISES: *Exercise 63, Ex. 60 (10-15)*
❏ CHECK: All your answers. ❏ REDO: Incorrect answers.
❏ DAILY FUN DRILL

You may do
Ex. 63 orally

Day 3

❏ EXERCISES: *Exercise 64, Ex. 60 (16-20)*
❏ CHECK: All your answers. ❏ REDO: Incorrect answers.
❏ DAILY FUN DRILL

Day 4

❏ EXERCISES: *Ex. 60 (21-27)*
❏ CHECK: All your answers. ❏ REDO: Incorrect answers.
❏ RECORD: Derivatives (Related English Words, p. 56) in derivative section of Latin notebook. Add *impetuous, exercise, adventure,*
❏ DAILY FUN DRILL

Day 5

❏ WEEKLY QUIZ

DAILY FUN DRILL:
    ❏ RECITE: *Pater Noster*, pp. 388-389; *Gloria Patri*, p. 118
    ❏ RECITE: All grammar forms: *terra, servus, bellum, lex, pars, flumen, portus*, case endings and the conjugation of *sum*
    ❏ DRILL: Vocabulary cards, grammar cards

❏ READ: *Lesson 4, No. 2, pp. 57-59*
VOCABULARY: *Text, p. 58*
    ❏ SAY: Vocabulary words aloud three times.
    ❏ WRITE: Vocabulary words three times.
    ❏ MAKE: Vocabulary cards.
    ❏ MAKE GRAMMAR CARD # 29
    ❏ RECORD: In **D** section of notebook, the Note on p. 59

❏ READ AGAIN: *Lesson 4, No. 2, pp. 57-59*
❏ EXERCISE: *Exercise 65 (1-8), pp. 59-60*
❏ CHECK: All your answers. ❏ REDO: Incorrect answers.
❏ DAILY FUN DRILL

❏ READ AGAIN: *Lesson 4, No. 2, pp. 57-59*
❏ EXERCISE: *Exercise 65 (9-11), Ex. 66, p. 60*
❏ CHECK: All your answers. ❏ REDO: Incorrect answers.
❏ DAILY FUN DRILL

❏ EXERCISE: *Exercise 67, p. 60.*
❏ CHECK: All your answers. ❏ REDO: Incorrect answers.
❏ DAILY FUN DRILL

❏ WEEKLY QUIZ

DAILY FUN DRILL:
    ❏ RECITE: *Pater Noster*, pp. 388-389; *Gloria Patri*, p. 118
    ❏ RECITE: All grammar forms: *terra, servus, bellum, lex, pars, flumen, portus,* case endings and the conjugation of *sum*
    ❏ DRILL: Vocabulary cards, grammar cards

Day 1

Students are likely to start making many mistakes with confusing verbs, such as *vicerunt* and *venerunt.* Make one drill card with *all* verbs from Vocabulary lists beginning on page 1. Drill these words orally until you know them automatically.

Day 2

Day 3

Day 4

Day 5

The 5th Declension (*res*)

LESSON 19

Congratulations, you have made it to the fifth declension. There are no more noun declensions to learn. Be sure to say all five declensions (eight model nouns, and the endings) every day.

Day 1

❏ READ: *Lesson 5, p. 62*
GRAMMAR: *Grammar, p. 13, No. 69, 70*
   ❏ SAY: Declension of *res* aloud, three times. Commit to memory
   ❏ RECORD: Declension of *res, Grammar 69,* in notebook.
   ❏ RECORD: Note in section **D** of Notebook.
   ❏ MAKE GRAMMAR CARDS # 30, 31
VOCABULARY: *Text, p. 62*
   ❏ SAY: Vocabulary words aloud three times.
   ❏ WRITE: Vocabulary words three times.
   ❏ MAKE: Vocabulary cards
❏ EXERCISES: *Exercises 69, 70, 71, pp. 61, 62*
❏ CHECK: All your answers. ❏ REDO: Incorrect answers.
❏ DAILY FUN DRILL

You may do
Ex. 71 orally

Day 2

❏ EXERCISES: *Exercises 72,73*
❏ CHECK: All your answers. ❏ REDO: Incorrect answers.
❏ DAILY FUN DRILL

Day 3

For Ex. 74 you do
not need to give
the rule for
1.

❏ EXERCISES: *Exercise 74, first half of Ex. 68*
❏ CHECK: All your answers. ❏ REDO: Incorrect answers.
❏ DAILY FUN DRILL

Day 4

❏ EXERCISES: *Second half of Ex. 68, p. 63*
❏ CHECK: All your answers. ❏ REDO: Incorrect answers.
❏ RECORD: Derivatives (Related English Words, p.62) in derivative section of Latin notebook. Add *despair*, *desperado*, and *sola fide* (by faith alone)
❏ DAILY FUN DRILL

Day 5

❏ WEEKLY QUIZ

DAILY FUN DRILL:
   ❏ RECITE: *Pater Noster*, pp. 388-389; *Gloria Patri*, p. 118
   ❏ RECITE: All grammar forms: *terra, servus, bellum, lex, pars, flumen portus, res,* case endings and the conjugation of *sum*
   ❏ DRILL: Vocabulary cards, grammar cards

GRAMMAR FORMS **Day 1**
❏ RECITE & WRITE: All noun declensions and case endings until you can do them perfectly from memory
VOCABULARY
❏ DRILL: Vocabulary cards orally until you know them—Latin to English and English to Latin--without error. You should know the gender of all nouns.
❏ WRITE: Using English side of vocab. cards, write Latin words including the genitive form with correct spellings.
TRANSLATION- Practice test
❏ COPY, CLOSE BOOK, AND TRANSLATE: # 5 from each of the following exercises: 6, 7, 8, 9, 13, 14, 16, 17, 18, 19, 20, 21.

GRAMMAR **Day 2**
❏ DRILL: All grammar cards until you know them without error.
❏ READ: Notes in Word Usage section of Notebook.
TRANSLATION - Practice test
❏ COPY, CLOSE BOOK, AND TRANSLATE: # 5 from each of the following exercises: 22, 23, 24, 25, 31, 32, 33, 34, 35, 36, 37, 38.

TRANSLATION—Practice test **Day 3**
❏ COPY, CLOSE BOOK, AND TRANSLATE: # 5 from each of the following exercises: 40, 41, 42, 45, 46, 47, 50, 51, 53, 54, 55, 56, 57

TRANSLATION—Practice Test **Day 4**
❏ COPY, CLOSE BOOK, AND TRANSLATE: # 5 from each of the following exercises: 59, 60, 61, 63, 64, 65, 66, 67 (5th sentence), 68 (5th sentence)72, 73

Day 5

TRANSLATION—TEST
❏ COPY, CLOSE BOOK, AND TRANSLATE: # 4 from each of the following exercises: 14, 19, 20, 36, 41, 46, 60, 57, 65, 72

Exercises 76-80
pp. 64-69

LESSON 21

The concept of plural nouns can be difficult. Think of *scissors*, *trousers*, or *woods*, English words that are plural but signify single things. Latin has many of these nouns and they often give students trouble. This is a hard week. Schedule plenty of time to complete your work

Day 1

Castra and *impedimenta* are neuter nouns of the 2nd declension. They are declined in the plural only, thus the declension of castra is: *castra, castrorum, castris, castra, castris.* Write the gender, number, and decl. of these nouns on your vocabulary cards.

Make separate cards for the singular and plural forms of *copia,* and *gratia.* Also make two cards for the two meanings of *gratia*: the classical meaning and the Christian one.

If you have an old key there is an error in Ex. 76. *In castra agmen cum impedimentis venit. The translation should be:* The column came into camp with the baggage train.

Day 3

Remember that these plural Latin nouns take **plural verbs in Latin.** But when they are translated **Day 4** into English, both the nouns verbs are singular.
So *castra sunt* is translated the *camp is.*

Day 5

❑ **READ:** *Unit 1, Lesson 6, p. 64, first paragraph only.* What is the gender of *castra* and *impedimenta*? What declension are they? In English we use a singular noun and a singular verb for *camp* and *baggage train*, but in Latin you have to use the plural verb with the plural noun. Decline castra and impedimenta.

❑ **READ:** *Unit 1, Lesson 6, pp. 64-65, next four vocabulary words.* There are only two words here, but they have different meaning in the singular and plural. Study them carefully.

❑ **READ:** *Unit 1, Lesson 6, pp. 64-65, next two vocabulary words.* These two verbs have special meanings with *castra,* **camp** and *gratias,* **thanks.**

VOCABULARY: *Text*, p. 64.

 ❑ **SAY:** Vocabulary words aloud three times.
 ❑ **WRITE:** Vocabulary words three times.
 ❑ **MAKE:** Vocabulary cards.
 ❑ **RECORD:** Notes about all words in Section **D** of notebook.

❑ **EXERCISE:** *Exercise 76, p. 66.*
❑ **CHECK:** All your answers. ❑ **REDO:** Incorrect answers.
❑ **DAILY FUN DRILL**

❑ **EXERCISE:** *Exercise 77, pp. 66-67.*
❑ **CHECK:** All your answers. ❑ **REDO:** Incorrect answers.
❑ **DAILY FUN DRILL**

❑ **EXERCISE:** *Exercise 78, 79, 80 p. 67 -69.*
❑ **CHECK:** All your answers. ❑ **REDO:** Incorrect answers.
❑ **DAILY FUN DRILL**

❑ **EXERCISE:** *Exercise 75 (1-5), p. 65.*
❑ **CHECK:** All your answers. ❑ **REDO:** Incorrect answers.
❑ **RECORD:** Derivatives (Related English Words, p. 65). Add *gratuitous, copious* and *impediment, Lancaster (many English towns were orginally Roman forts) and cornucopia.* .
❑ **DAILY FUN DRILL**

❑ **WEEKLY QUIZ**

DAILY FUN DRILL:
 ❑ **RECITE:** *Pater Noster*, pp. 388-389; *Gloria Patri,* p. 118; *Anima Christi,* p. 365
 ❑ **RECITE:** All grammar forms: *terra, servus, bellum, lex, pars, flumen portus, res,* case endings and the conjugation of *sum*
 ❑ **DRILL:** Vocabulary cards, grammar cards

❏ READ AGAIN: *Unit 1, Lesson 6, "Nouns with Special Meanings in the Plural," pp. 64-65.*
❏ EXERCISE: *Exercise 75, 6,7,8 (1/2), p. 65.*
❏ CHECK: All your answers. ❏ REDO: Incorrect answers.
❏ DAILY FUN DRILL

Day 1

❏ EXERCISE: Exercise 75, #8 (1/2) , p. 65.
❏ CHECK: All your answers. ❏ REDO: Incorrect answers.
❏ DAILY FUN DRILL

Day 2

❏ EXERCISE: *Exercise 81, (1-11), p. 70*
❏ CHECK: All your answers. ❏ REDO: Incorrect answers.
❏ DAILY FUN DRILL

Day 3

❏ EXERCISE: *Exercise 81, (12-22) p. 70*
❏ CHECK: All your answers. ❏ REDO: Incorrect answers.
❏ DAILY FUN DRILL

Day 4

❏ WEEKLY QUIZ

Day 5

DAILY FUN DRILL:
   ❏ RECITE: *Pater Noster*, pp. 388-389; *Gloria Patri*, p. 118; *Anima Christi*, p. 365
   ❏ RECITE: All grammar forms: *terra, servus, bellum, lex, pars, flumen portus, res,* case endings and the conjugation of *sum*
   ❏ DRILL: Vocabulary cards, grammar cards

Exercises 81-83
pp. 70-71

LESSON 23

This week is a review of all of Unit One. Do all the exercises carefully and correctly before you move on to the next unit.

Day 1
❏ EXERCISE: *Exercise 81, (23-44), p. 70.*
❏ CHECK: All your answers. ❏ REDO: Incorrect answers.
❏ DAILY FUN DRILL

Day 2
❏ EXERCISE: *Exercise 82, p. 70.*
❏ CHECK: All your answers. ❏ REDO: Incorrect answers.
❏ DAILY FUN DRILL

Day 3
❏ EXERCISE: *Exercise 83, nos. 1-20, p. 71.*
❏ CHECK: All your answers. ❏ REDO: Incorrect answers.
❏ DAILY FUN DRILL

Day 4
❏ EXERCISE: *Exercise 83, nos. 21-36, p. 71.*
❏ CHECK: All your answers. ❏ REDO: Incorrect answers.
❏ DAILY FUN DRILL

Day 5
❏ WEEKLY QUIZ

DAILY FUN DRILL:
❏ RECITE: *Pater Noster*, pp. 388-389; *Gloria Patri*, p. 118; *Anima Christi*, p. 365
❏ RECITE: All grammar forms: *terra, servus, bellum, lex, pars, flumen portus, res,* case endings and the conjugation of *sum*
❏ DRILL: Vocabulary cards, grammar cards

There are two groups of adjectives: (1) 1st/2nd Declension Adjectives (2) 3rd Declension Adjectives. Each group has all three genders. If you do not know the gender of each noun you will not be able to write the adjectives correctly.

Day 1

❏ READ: *Unit 2, Lesson 1, No. 1, p. 72 & No. 2, p. 73.*
GRAMMAR:
   ❏ RECORD: The declension of *magnus, Grammar,* No. 72.
   ❏ MAKE GRAMMAR CARDS # 32, 33.
VOCABULARY: *Text,* p. 73.
   ❏ SAY: Vocabulary words aloud three times.
   ❏ WRITE: Vocabulary words three times.
   ❏ MAKE: Vocabulary cards.
   ❏ RECORD: Note on p. 74 in Section **D** of Notebook.
❏ EXERCISE: *Exercise 84, p. 74*
❏ CHECK: All your answers. ❏ REDO: Incorrect answers.
❏ DAILY FUN DRILL

The difficult concepts with these adjectives are 1) they are written in all three genders (2) they modify nouns in the other declensions.

Day 2

❏ READ AGAIN: *Unit 2, Lesson 1, No. 1, p. 72 & No. 2, p. 73.*
❏ READ: *Unit 2, Lesson 1, p. 74.*
   ❏ MAKE GRAMMAR CARD # 34.
❏ EXERCISE: *Exercise 85, pp. 74-75.*
❏ CHECK: All your answers. ❏ REDO: Incorrect answers.
❏ DAILY FUN DRILL

Day 3

❏ READ AGAIN: *Unit 2, Lesson 1, pp. 72-74*
❏ EXERCISE: *Exercise 86, p. 75*
❏ CHECK: All your answers. ❏ REDO: Incorrect answers.
❏ DAILY FUN DRILL

Day 4

❏ EXERCISE: *Exercise 87, p. 75*
❏ CHECK: All your answers. ❏ REDO: Incorrect answers.
❏ RECORD: Derivatives on p. 73. Add: *magnify, bonny, longitude, malice, multitude, sanctity, sanctify, primary,* and *prime.*
❏ DAILY FUN DRILL

❏ WEEKLY QUIZ

Day 5

DAILY FUN DRILL:
   ❏ RECITE: *Pater Noster,* pp. 388-389; *Gloria Patri,* p. 118; *Anima Christi,* p. 365
   ❏ RECITE: All grammar forms: *terra, servus, bellum, lex, pars, flumen portus, res, magnus,* case endings and the conjugation of *sum*
   ❏ DRILL: Vocabulary cards, grammar cards

Exercises 88-89, 91
pp. 75-79

LESSON 25

Day 1

Be careful with this
exercise. Get all of your
adjective endings correct.

❏ READ: *Unit 2, Lesson 1, No. 3, pp. 75-76.*
GRAMMAR:
   ❏ RECORD: In grammar section of notebook, the difference between
   predicate adjectives and attributive adjectives.
   ❏ MAKE GRAMMAR CARD # 35:
VOCABULARY: *Text*, p. 76.
   ❏ SAY: Vocabulary words aloud three times.
   ❏ WRITE: Vocabulary words three times.
   ❏ MAKE: Vocabulary cards.
❏ EXERCISE: *Exercise 88, pp. 76-77*
❏ CHECK: All your answers. ❏ REDO: Incorrect answers.
❏ DAILY FUN DRILL

Day 2

Remember *pro* always takes
the ablative and there are
two meanings: *in front of*
and *on behalf of (for)*.

Do not confuse *propter*
(on account of) with *pro*
(on behalf of).

Copia and *inopia* are
opposites.

❏ READ AGAIN: *Unit 2, Lesson 1, No. 3, pp. 75-76.*
❏ READ: *Unit 2, Lesson 1, No. 4, p. 77.*
VOCABULARY: *Text*, p. 78.
   ❏ SAY: Vocabulary words aloud three times.
   ❏ WRITE: Vocabulary words three times.
   ❏ MAKE: Vocabulary cards.
❏ EXERCISE: *Exercise 89, p. 78.*
❏ CHECK: All your answers. ❏ REDO: Incorrect answers.
❏ DAILY FUN DRILL

Day 3

❏ READ AGAIN: *Unit 2, Lesson 1, No. 4, pp. 77-78*
❏ EXERCISE: *Exercise 90 (1/2) , p. 79.*
❏ CHECK: All your answers. ❏ REDO: Incorrect answers.
❏ DECLINE: all of the adjectives in the vocabulary, p. 76.
❏ DAILY FUN DRILL

Day 4

❏ EXERCISE: *Exercise 90 (1/2) , p. 79.*
❏ RECORD: Derivatives (Related English Words), p. 76.
❏ DAILY FUN DRILL

Day 5

❏ WEEKLY QUIZ

DAILY FUN DRILL:
   ❏ RECITE: *Pater Noster*, pp. 388-389; *Gloria Patri*, p. 118; *Anima
Christi*, p. 365
   ❏ RECITE: All grammar forms: *terra, servus, bellum, lex, pars, flumen
portus, res, magnus,* case endings and the conjugation of *sum*
   ❏ DRILL: Vocabulary cards, grammar cards

Extra Credit

❏ Translate the two boxed sayings on pp. 77 & 78. Explain the case of all nouns
and adjectives in both sayings.

Day 1

Be sure you can identify
the subject of the sentence
in English before trying to
translate it into Latin.

Day 2

In # 7, a noun and its
adjective are frequently
separated by a genitive
(*magna frumenti inopia-*
a large scarcity of grain)

Day 3

Day 4

Day 5

Extra Credit

❏ READ AGAIN: *Unit 2, Lesson 1, No. 4, pp. 77-78.*
❏ EXERCISE: *Exercise 91, p. 79.*
❏ CHECK: All your answers. ❏ REDO: Incorrect answers.
❏ DAILY FUN DRILL

❏ EXERCISE: *Exercise 92, p. 80.*
❏ CHECK: All your answers. ❏ REDO: Incorrect answers.
❏ DAILY FUN DRILL

❏ EXERCISE: *Exercise 93, p. 80.*
❏ CHECK: All your answers. ❏ REDO: Incorrect answers.
❏ DECLINE: All nouns and adjectives in vocabulary, p. 78.
❏ DAILY FUN DRILL

❏ EXERCISE: *Exercise 94, p. 81.*
❏ CHECK: All your answers. ❏ REDO: Incorrect answers.
❏ RECORD: Derivatives (Related English Words), p. 78.
❏ DAILY FUN DRILL

❏ WEEKLY QUIZ

DAILY FUN DRILL:
    ❏ RECITE: *Pater Noster*, pp. 388-389; *Gloria Patri*, p. 118; *Anima Christi*, p. 365
    ❏ RECITE: All grammar forms: *terra, servus, bellum, lex, pars, flumen portus, res, magnus*, case endings and the conjugation of *sum*
    ❏ DRILL: Vocabulary cards, grammar cards

❏ Translate boxed sayings on pp. 79-81. Identify cases of all nouns.

This is the last adjective declension you have to learn. It is a little frustrating to have to remember the minor differences between the 3rd declension noun and adjective forms, but with daily recitation you will master them in no time.

Day 1

Here is an old trick: when declining *gravis,* stand up when you say the ablative singular. It will help you remember that the **i** in the adjective forms is different from the **e** in the noun forms.

❏ READ: *Unit 2, Lesson 8, No. 1, p. 82.*
GRAMMAR:
  ❏ RECORD: Declension of *gravis, Grammar,* No. 78.
  ❏ RECORD: In grammar section of Notebook, the three observations on the declension of *gravis* on p. 82.
VOCABULARY: *Text, p. 82.*
  ❏ SAY: Vocabulary words aloud three times.
  ❏ WRITE: Vocabulary words three times.
  ❏ MAKE: Vocabulary cards.
❏ EXERCISE: *Exercise 95, nos. 1-3, pp. 83.*
❏ CHECK: All your answers. ❏ REDO: Incorrect answers.
❏ DAILY FUN DRILL

Day 2

❏ READ AGAIN: *Unit 2, Lesson 8, No. 1, p. 82.*
❏ EXERCISE: *Exercise 95, nos. 4-5, pp. 83.*
❏ CHECK: All your answers. ❏ REDO: Incorrect answers.
❏ DAILY FUN DRILL

Day 3

❏ EXERCISE: *Exercise 96, p. 84.*
❏ CHECK: All your answers. ❏ REDO: Incorrect answers.
❏ DECLINE: all of the adjectives orally in the vocabulary, p. 82.
❏ DAILY FUN DRILL

Day 4

❏ RECORD: Derivatives (Related English Words), p. 83. Add: *abbreviate, brevity, facility, gravity, communal, communion, omnibus,* and *fortitude*.
❏ EXERCISE: *Exercise 97, 1-9, p. 84.*
❏ CHECK: All your answers. ❏ REDO: Incorrect answers.
❏ DAILY FUN DRILL

Day 5

❏ EXERCISE: *Exercise 97, 10-17, p. 84.*
❏ CHECK: All your answers. ❏ REDO: Incorrect answers.
❏ WEEKLY QUIZ

DAILY FUN DRILL:
  ❏ RECITE: *Pater Noster,* pp. 388-389; *Gloria Patri,* p. 118; *Anima Christi,* p. 365
  ❏ RECITE: All grammar forms: *terra, servus, bellum, lex, pars, flumen portus, res, magnus, gravis,* case endings and the conjugation of *sum*
  ❏ DRILL: Vocabulary cards, grammar cards

Read this grammar lesson several times before you try to do this lesson. This lesson is about adjectives that are modified by prepositional phrases in both English and Latin. The difficulty is that in Latin the prepositional phrase is expressed by the prepositional object in the appropriate case *without* the preposition. One of the big differences between English and Latin is that the relationships between words are often indicated by cases rather than by prepositions.

❏ READ: *Unit 2, Lesson 8, No. 2, p. 85.*
VOCABULARY: *Text, p. 85.*
   ❏ SAY: Vocabulary words aloud three times.
   ❏ WRITE: Vocabulary words three times.
   ❏ MAKE: Vocabulary cards.
❏ EXERCISE: *Exercise 98, p. 86.*
❏ CHECK: All your answers. ❏ REDO: Incorrect answers.
❏ DAILY FUN DRILL

❏ READ AGAIN: *Unit 2, Lesson 8, No. 2, p. 85.*
❏ EXERCISE: *Exercise 99, p. 87.*
❏ CHECK: All your answers. ❏ REDO: Incorrect answers.
❏ DAILY FUN DRILL

❏ READ AGAIN: *Unit 2, Lesson 8, No. 2, p. 85.*
❏ READ: *Unit 2, Lesson 8, No. 3, p. 87, 88.*
VOCABULARY: *Text, p. 87.*
   ❏ SAY: Vocabulary words aloud three times.
   ❏ WRITE: Vocabulary words three times.
   ❏ MAKE: Vocabulary cards.
GRAMMAR:
   ❏ RECORD: Declension of *Jesus*, p. 87.
   ❏ RECORD: *Notes p. 87, 88* in section D of Notebook.
❏ EXERCISE: *Exercise 100, p. 88.*
❏ CHECK: All your answers. ❏ REDO: Incorrect answers.
❏ DECLINE: All nouns and adjectives in vocabularies, pp. 85 and 87.
❏ DAILY FUN DRILL

❏ RECORD: *Derivatives (Related English Words), pp. 86 and 88.*
❏ EXERCISE: *Exercise 101, p. 88.*
❏ DAILY FUN DRILL

❏ WEEKLY QUIZ
DAILY FUN DRILL:
   ❏ RECITE: *Pater Noster*, pp. 388-389; *Gloria Patri*, p. 118; *Anima Christi*, p. 365
   ❏ RECITE: All grammar forms: *terra, servus, bellum, lex, pars, flumen portus, res, magnus, gravis*, case endings and the conjugation of *sum*
   ❏ DRILL: Vocabulary cards, grammar cards

❏ Translate boxed saying on p. 88. Explain the form of *Jesu*.
HENLE LATIN STUDY GUIDE

Day 1
These sentences are a little tricky. In # 1, Ex. 98, *cupidi* is a predicate adjective agreeing with the subject, *Galli*. *Gloriae* means *of glory* and modifies *cupidi*. If you will diagram these sentences in English and Latin you will understand them better.

Day 2

Day 3

Urbs and *pons* are **i stem** nouns. Be sure to record that on your vocab card. Also that *pons* is M. There are three exceptions to the SOX rule this year: *mons, pons,* and *collis.*

Day 4

Day 5

Extra Credit

Exercises 102-103
pp. 88-90

LESSON 29

Day 1
- ❏ READ AGAIN: *pp. 87-88*
- ❏ EXERCISE: *Exercise 102, p. 89.*
- ❏ CHECK: All your answers. ❏ REDO: Incorrect answers.
- ❏ DAILY FUN DRILL

Day 2
- ❏ EXERCISE: *Exercise 103 (1-4), p. 90*
- ❏ CHECK: All your answers. ❏ REDO: Incorrect answers.
- ❏ DAILY FUN DRILL

Day 3
- ❏ EXERCISE: *Exercise 103, (5-7), p. 90*
- ❏ CHECK: All your answers. ❏ REDO: Incorrect answers.
- ❏ DAILY FUN DRILL

Day 4
- ❏ EXERCISE: *Exercise 103, 8-12, p. 90.*
- ❏ CHECK: All your answers. ❏ REDO: Incorrect answers.
- ❏ DAILY FUN DRILL

Day 5
- ❏ TRANSLATE: *Reading No. 3, p. 90.*
- ❏ WEEKLY QUIZ

DAILY FUN DRILL:
- ❏ RECITE: *Pater Noster*, pp. 388-389; *Gloria Patri*, p. 118; *Anima Christi*, p. 365
- ❏ RECITE: All grammar forms: *terra, servus, bellum, lex, pars, flumen portus, res, magnus, gravis,* case endings and the conjugation of *sum*
- ❏ DRILL: Vocabulary cards, grammar cards

Extra Credit
- ❏ Translate boxed saying on p. 90. Explain cases of nouns.

If you have reviewed, drilled and corrected all of your work carefully all year you should be able to complete day 1 in a very short time and make and A on your final.

Use the Mastery Review on pages 91-98 as an additional aid for review if you need to.

GRAMMAR FORMS   **Day 1**
❏ RECITE & WRITE: All noun declensions and case endings until you can do them perfectly from memory
❏ READ: All grammar and word usage notes in Notebook.
❏ DRILL: All grammar cards until you know them without error.
VOCABULARY
❏ DRILL: Vocabulary cards orally until you know them--Latin to English and English to Latin--without error. You should know the gender of all nouns and the case each preposition takes.
❏ WRITE: Using English side of vocab. cards, write Latin words including the genitive form with correct spellings.

TRANSLATION- Practice test   **Day 2**
❏ COPY, CLOSE BOOK, AND TRANSLATE: # 5 from each of the following exercises: 75, 83, 84, 85, 86, 87, 88, 89, 91, 92

TRANSLATION—Practice test   **Day 3**
❏ COPY, CLOSE BOOK, AND TRANSLATE: # 5 from each of the following exercises: 93, 94, 96, 97, 98, 99, 101, 103 (# 5, 11, 12)

TRANSLATION—Practice test   **Day 4**
❏ COPY, CLOSE BOOK, AND TRANSLATE: # 3 or sentence 3 from each of the following exercises: 75, 76, 77, 80, 83, 84, 85, 90, 100, 102.

TRANSLATION—TEST   **Day 5**
❏ COPY, CLOSE BOOK, AND TRANSLATE:# 4 or sentence #4 from each of the following exercises: 75, 76, 77, 80, 83, 84 (# 4, 24, 29, 30), 85, 86, 87, 88, 89, 91, 92, 93, 94, 95, 96, 97, 99, 101, 102, 103

1. How do you know when a noun is in the 1st declension?

2. Decline *terra, ae.*

3. Give the gender rules for the 1st declension.

4. What is the case of the subject of a (finite) verb?

5. How does a (finite) verb agree with its subject?

6. What is the case of the object of a transitive verb?

7. Where does a verb usually stands in a sentence?

8. Where does an adverb usually stands in a sentence?

9. Name the case into which possessives and English *of-* phrases are translated in Latin.

10. How do you know when a noun is in the 2nd declension?

11. Give the gender rules for the 2nd declension

12. Decline *servus, i.*

13. Decline *bellum, i.*

14. What distinguishes the declension of *servus* and *bellum*?

15. Give the gender rules for nouns in the 2nd declension like *servus.*

16. Give the gender rules for 2nd declension nouns like *bellum.*

17. Which case is the case of the indirect object?

---

1. You know a noun is in the 1st declension when

_____

2.   _____   _____
      _____   _____
      _____   _____
      _____   _____
      _____   _____

3. All nouns in the 1st declension are _____ unless they name an individual _____ person.

4. The subject of a (finite) verb is in the _____ case.

5. A (finite) verb agrees with its subject in _____ and _____.

6. The object of a transtitive verb is in the _____ case.

7. The verb usually stands _____ in a sentence.

8. Adverbs usually stand immediately _____ the word they modify.

9. English possessives and many of-phrases are translated into the Latin _____.

10. You know a noun is in the 2nd declension when its _____ _____ ends in _____.

11. In the 2nd declension, masculine nouns have a ____ ending in the nominative singular, while neuter nouns have a ___ ending in the nominative singular.

12.   _____   _____
      _____   _____
      _____   _____
      _____   _____
      _____   _____

13.   _____   _____
      _____   _____
      _____   _____
      _____   _____
      _____   _____

14. In the declension of neuter nouns like *bellum*, the endings in the nominative and accusative singular and plural are always _____.

15. Nouns in the 2nd declension like *servus* are generally _____.

16. Nouns in the 2nd declension like *bellum* are _____.

17. The indirect object is put in the _____ case.

18. Name the two cases in which nouns are put when they follow Latin prepositions.

18. Nouns that follow Latin prepositions are put in the _____ or _____ cases.

19. Name the case into which the predicate noun is put after a linking verb.

19. A predicate noun is put in the same case as the _____ (the _____ case).

20. Conjugate *sum*.

20. _____ _____
    _____ _____
    _____ _____

21. Where do forms of the word *sum* stand in the sentence?

21. Forms of the word *sum* can stand _____ in the sentence.

22. How you know when a noun is in the 3rd declension?

22. A noun is in the 3rd declension when its _____ _____ ending is ____.

23. Decline *lex*.

23. _____ _____
    _____ _____
    _____ _____
    _____ _____
    _____ _____

24. Give the gender rules for nouns in the 3rd declension.

24. **Step #1:** If _____, then _____; and if _____ _____, then _____.

    Step #2: If neither of these conditions apply, then _____.

25. Give the SOX rule.

25. The SOX rule states that if the nominative singular form of a 3rd declension noun ends in __, __ or __, then it is _____.

26. Give the ERROR rule.

26. The ERROR rule states that if the nominative singular form of a 3rd declension noun ends in ___ or ___, then it is _____.

27. Give the LANCET rule.

27. The LANCET rule states that if the nominative singular form of a 3rd declension noun ends in __, __, __, __, __ or __, then it is _____.

28. Decline *pars*.

28. _____ _____
    _____ _____
    _____ _____
    _____ _____
    _____ _____

29. [Optional] When is a 3rd declension masculine or feminine noun declined like *pars* rather than *lex?*

29. A 3rd declension masculine or feminine noun should be declined like pars when either of the two following conditions are met:
    Condition #1: When the last two letters of the stem are _____.

    Condition #2: When the nominative and genitive singular have the same number of _____.

30. What is an appositive?

30. An appositive is a _____ or _____ that renames or describes another _____ or _____ and is set next to it and often set off with _____.

31. Give the rule of agreement for appositives.

31. An appositive agrees with its noun in _____ and _____.

32. Decline *flumen.*

32. _____ _____
    _____ _____
    _____ _____
    _____ _____
    _____ _____

33. Decline *portus, us.*

33. _____ _____
    _____ _____
    _____ _____
    _____ _____
    _____ _____

34. How do you know when a noun is in the 4th declension?

34. A noun is in the 4th declension when its _____ _____ ending is ___.

35. Decline *res, ei.*

35. _____ _____
    _____ _____
    _____ _____
    _____ _____
    _____ _____

36. How do you know when a noun is in the 5th declension?

36. A noun is in the 5th declension when it _____ _____ ending is ___.

37. Decline *magnus, -a, -um.*

37. _____ _____ _____
Sing. _____ _____ _____
    _____ _____ _____
    _____ _____ _____

    _____ _____ _____
Pl. _____ _____ _____
    _____ _____ _____
    _____ _____ _____

38. Give the rule of agreement for adjectives.

38. Adjectives agree with the nouns they modify in _____, _____ and _____.

39. Give the rule for the position of adjectives according to quantity and quality.

39. An adjective of _____ generally precedes its noun; an adjective of _____ generally follows its noun.

40. Decline *gravis, -e.*

40. _____ _____ _____
Sing. _____ _____ _____
    _____ _____ _____
    _____ _____ _____

    _____ _____ _____
Pl. _____ _____ _____
    _____ _____ _____
    _____ _____ _____

1. You know a noun is in the 1st declension when **its genitive singular ends in -*ae***

2. **terra, terrae, terrae, terram, terra, terrae, terrarum, terris, terras, terris**

3. All nouns in the 1st declension are **feminine** unless they name an individual **male** person.

4. The subject of a (finite) verb is in the **nominative** case.

5. A (finite) verb agrees with its subject in **number** and **person.**

6. The object of a verb is in the **accusative** case.

7. The verb usually stands **last** in a sentence.

8. Adverbs usually stand immediately **before** the word they modify.

9. English possessives and many *of*-phrases are translated into the Latin **genitive**.

10. You know a noun is in the 2nd declension when its **genitive singular** ends in -*i*

11. In the 2nd declension, masculine nouns have a **-*us*** ending in the nominative singular, while neuter nouns have a **-*um*** ending in the nominative singular.

12. **servus, servi, servo, servum, servo, servi, servorum, servis, servos, servis**

13. **bellum, belli, bello, bellum, bello, bella, bellorum, bellis bella, bellis**

14. In the declension of neuter nouns like *bellum*, the ending in the nominative and accusative singular and plural is always **the same.**

15. Nouns in the 2nd declension like *serv*us are generally **masculine.**

16. Nouns in the 2nd declension like *bellum* are **neuter.**

17. The indirect object is put in the **dative** case.

18. Nouns that follow Latin prepositions are put in the **accusative** or **ablative** cases.

19. A predicate noun is put in the same case as the **subject** (the **nominative case**).

20. **sum, es, est, sumus, estis, sunt**

21. Forms of the word *sum* can stand **anywhere** in the sentence.

22. A noun is in the 3rd declension when its **genitive singular** ending is -*is*.

23. **lex, legis, legi, legem, lege, leges, legum, legibus, leges, legibus**

24. **Step #1:** If **the noun names an individual male person**, then **it is masculine**; and if **it names an individual female person**, then **it is feminine.**
    Step #2: If neither of these conditions apply, then **apply the SOX, ERROR, or LANCET rules.**

25. The SOX rule states that if the nominative singular form of a 3rd declension noun ends in -*s*, -*o* or -*x*, then it is **feminine.**

26. The ERROR rule states that if the nominative singular form of a 3rd declension noun ends in *-er* or *-or*, then it is **masculine**.

27. The LANCET rule states that if the nominative singular form of a 3rd declension noun ends in *-l*, *-a*, *-n*, *-c*, *-e* or *-t*, then it is **neuter**.

28. **pars, partis, parti, partem, parte, partes, partium, partibus, partes, partibus**

29. A 3rd declension masculine or feminine noun should be declined like pars when **either** of the two following conditions apply:
    Condition #1: When the last two letters of the stem are **consonants**.
    Condition #2: When the nominative and genitive singular have the same number of **syllables**.

30. An appositive is a **noun** or **phrase** that renames or describes another **noun** or **phrase** and is set next to it and often set off with **commas**.

31. An appositive agrees with its noun in **number** and **case**.

32. **flumen, fluminis, flumini, flumen, flumine, flumina, fluminum, fluminibus, flumina, fluminibus**

33. **portus, portus, portui, portum, portu, portus, portuum, portibus, portus, portibus**

34. A noun is in the 4th declension when its **genitive singular** ending is *-us*.

35. **res, rei, rei, rem, re, res, rerum, rebus, res, rebus**

36. A noun is in the 5th declension when its **genitive singular** ending is *-ei*.

37. **M: magnus, magni, magno, magnum, magno, magni, magnorum, magnis, magnos, magnis**
    F: magna, magnae, magnae, magnam, magna, magnae, magnarum, magnis, magnas, magnis
    N: magnum, magni, magno, magnum magno, magna, magnorum, magnis, magna, magnis

38. Adjectives agree with the nouns they modify in **gender**, **number** and **case**.

39. An adjective of **quantity** generally precedes its noun; an adjective of **quality** generally follows its noun.

40. **M: gravis, gravis, gravi, gravem, gravi, graves, gravium, gravibus, graves, gravibus**
    F: gravis, gravis, gravi, gravem, gravi, graves, gravium, gravibus, graves, gravibus
    N: grave, gravis, gravi, grave, gravi, gravia, gravium, gravibus, gravia, gravibus

HENLE LATIN KEY (UNITS I & II)

This key is intended as an aid to the busy teacher. It should serve to unlock readily and speedily whatever may be difficult or obscure. A few points in connection with the key and its use merit a word of comment.

1. In the English translations of Latin exercises the literal meanings of Latin words and sentences are usually given, since the main purpose is to make the Latin text clear rather than to give an example of good style. Occasionally (especially when a literal translation results in pidgin English) a freer translation is added in parentheses. While it may often be necessary to demand a literal translation first in order to make the meaning and the sentence structure clear, the final translation accepted by the teacher should always be pure, idiomatic English.

2. In translating English exercises into Latin this key seldom gives more than one version. "You" could often be either singular or plural; "they put" could be present, imperfect, or perfect; "I see" can be translated by three or more verbs. It would have been impossible to give every variant translation, nor would any useful purpose have been served by so doing.

3. Certain extremely simple exercises involving nothing more than knowledge of word meanings and syntactical forms are left unanswered. It was also considered unnecessary to diagram the sentences which the pupil is instructed to diagram, as all such sentences follow the simple models given in FIRST YEAR LATIN.

4. The English translations of passages from the New Testament are from the 1941 edition of the Confraternity of Christian Doctrine, published by St. Anthony Guild Press.

5. Numerical references such as "See No..." are in all cases without exception, to the author's LATIN GRAMMAR.

Exercise 1

porta, portae, portae, portam, porta, portae, portarum, portis, portas, portis

Maria, Mariae, Mariae, Mariam, Maria, Mariae, Mariarum, Mariis, Marias, Mariis

nauta, nautae, nautae, nautam, nauta, nautae, nautarum, nautis, nautas, nautis

victoria, victoriae, victoriae, victoriam, victoria, victoriae, victoriarum, victoriis, victorias, victoriis

silva, silvae, silvae, silvam, silva, silvae, silvarum, silvis, silvas, silvis

gloria, gloriae, gloriae, gloriam, gloria, gloriae, gloriarum, gloriis, glorias, gloriis

Exercise 2

1. accusative singular; land, earth
2. accusative plural; forests
3. genitive plural; of the gates
4. acc. S.; glory
5. acc. Pl.; gates
6. acc. S.; forest
7. gen. S., dat., S., nom. PL.; of the victory, to/for the victory, victories.
8. gen. Pl., of the sailors
9. gen., dat., S., nom. Pl.; of the land, to/for the land, lands.
10. nom. S., victory

See No. 31, p. 5 in Grammar for remaining answers.

Exercise 3

1. The final *a* of the nominative is short; of the ablative, long.
2. By dropping the case ending of the genitive singular.
3. By the genitive singular.

Exercise 4

All are feminine except *nauta, nautae,* which is masculine because it names a male person.

Exercise 5

1. Mary prays.
2. The sailors pray.
3. The sailor prays.
4. The sailors do not pray.
5. They see.
6. The sailor sees.
7. Mary sees.
8. He (she) sees.
9. The sailors do not see.
10. He (she) does not pray.

Exercise 6

1. The sailors praise the land.
2. The sailors see the province.
3. Mary praises the forests.
4. The sailor sees the forests.
5. The sailor sees the gate.
6. They do not praise the province.

7. The sailors praise Mary.
8. They praise the victory.
9. The sailors praise fame.
10. He (she) praises Mary.
11. He (she) sees the province.

Exercise 7
1. Marīam laudant.
2. Nautae prōvinciam vident.
3. Nautae glōriam laudant.
4. Portam videt.
5. Nauta prōvinciam nōn laudat.
6. Silvam laudant.
7. Nautās videt.
8. Victōriam laudat.
9. Portam vident.
10. Marīa nautās nōn laudat.
11. Nautae terram vident.

Exercise 8
1. The glory (fame) of the province.
2. The sailor's victory (the victory of the sailor).
3. Mary's glory (fame).
4. The sailor's glory (fame).
5. The forest of the province.
6. The sailors' victory.
7. The gate of the province.

Exercise 9
1. Victōria nautae.
2. Victōria Marīae.
3. Porta prōvinciae.
4. Glōria Marīae.
5. Victōria nautārum.
6. Silva prōvinciae.

Exercise 10
fīlius, filii, filio, filium, filio, fīlii, filiorum, filiis, fīlios, filiis
Deus, Dei, Deo, Deum, Deo
amicus, amici, amico, amicum, amico, amici, amicorum, amicis, amicos, amicis
etc.

Exercise 11
1. nom.,S.; God
2. acc., Pl. slaves,
3. dat., abl., Pl.; to/for the sons, by/with/from the sons
4. acc., S.; Christ
5. nom. S.; friend
6. acc., S. God
7. dat., abl., Pl.; to/for the friends, by/with/from the friends

See No. 34, p. 6 in Grammar for remaining answers.

Exercise 12
1. The glory of God.
2. The friend of the slave.
3. The friend of God.
4. The victory of God.
5. The glory of Christ.
6. The glory of Mary.
7. The victory of the Christians.
8. The servant of God.
9. The friend of Christ.
10. The Son of God.

Exercise 13
1. The Christians pray.
2. The friends of God praise the Christians.
3. The Christians praise the Son of God.
4. The Christians praise Mary.
5. The sailors do not see the slaves.
6. The slaves praise the Christians.
7. The Christians praise the servants of God.
8. They see the glory of God.
9. The Christians praise Christ.
10. Mary and Christ praise the friends of God.
11. God sees the land and the forests. He sees the sailors, the slaves, and the Christians.
12. The Christians praise the Son of Mary.

Exercise 14
1. Chrīstiānī Fīlium Marīae laudant.
2. Marīa Deī Fīlium videt.
3. Chrīstiānī Chrīstī victōriam laudant.
4. Marīa Deum laudat.
5. Deus glōriam Chrīstī laudat.
6. Chrīstus amīcōs Marīae laudat.
7. Marīae servī Chrīstum laudant.
8. Deī amīcī Marīam laudant.
9. Nautae servōrum victōriam nōn laudant.
10. Marīa Deī glōriam et Chrīstī victōriam videt.
11. Deus terram videt; silvās videt.

Exercise 15
1. dat., abl. S.; to/for heaven, by/with/from heaven
2. gen., Pl.; of the dangers
3. dat., abl. Pl.; to/for dangers, by/with/from dangers
4. dat., abl. S.; to/for power, by/with/from power
5. dat., abl. Pl.; to/for wars, by/with/from wars
6. gen., S.; of the danger
7. dat., abl. Pl.; to/for rewards, by/with/from rewards

8. gen., S.; of the kingdom
9. nom., acc., S.; command, power, empire
10. nom., acc., Pl.; wars
11. dat., abl. S.; to/for kingdom, by/with/from kingdom
12. nom., acc., Pl.; rewards

Exercise 16
1. The kingdom of Christ.
2. The danger of the servants.
3. The power of God.
4. The rewards of a Christian.
5. The gate of heaven.
6. The reward of Mary.
7. The danger of the friend.
8. The victory of Christ.

Exercise 17
1. The friends of God praise the kingdom of Christ.
2. Mary sees the reward and victory of Christ.
3. The sailors see the sky and the earth.
4. God sees the dangers of Christians.
5. God does not praise wars.
6. The servants of Christ praise the empire of Christ.
7. Mary sees the glory of the kingdom of Christ.
8. The Son of God praises the rewards of Mary.
9. The sailors do not praise the dangers of war.

Exercise 18
1. As follows
   (a) Nauta, m., No. 32. (Grammar, p. 5)
   (b) Porta, f., No. 33.
   (c) Rēgnum, n., No. 38.
   (d) Chrīstus, m., No. 35.
   (e) Marīa, f., No. 33.
   (f) Praemium, n., No. 38.
2. See Nos. 9-10.
3. Adverbs usually come before the words they modify; verbs usually stand last in the sentence.
4. The nominative is short, the ablative long.

Exercise 19
1. Christ gave glory to God.
2. They did not give swords to the slaves but they gave swords to the sailors.
3. The sailors gave victory to (their) friends.
4. God gave rewards to the friends of Mary.
5. God gave royal power to (His) Son.
6. The Christians gave glory to Mary and to the Son of Mary.
7. God gave the earth to Christ.

8. The sailors praise the glory of war but they do not praise the dangers of war. (No indirect object.)
9. He gave the province to (his) friend.
10. God gave glory and victory to the Christians.
11. He gave the sword to a friend.

Exercise 20
1. Deus Chrīstō rēgnum dedit.
2. Gladium amīcō dedit sed nōn servō.
3. Chrīstiānī glōriam Deō dedērunt.
4. Servīs prōvinciam nōn dedērunt.
5. Deī Fīlius Caelum Chrīstiānīs dedit.
6. Nautae perīcula bellī nōn laudant sed victōriam et praemia bellī laudant.
7. Deus rēgnum et imperium Chrīstō dedit.
8. Nautae caelum vident.

Exercise 21
1. Chrīstiānus ōrat. The Christian prays.
2. Chrīstiānī ōrant. The Christians pray.
3. Marīa Deum videt. Mary sees God.
4. Nautae terram vident. The sailors see the land.
5. Servus Chrīstī Caelum laudat. The servant of Christ praises heaven.
6. Amīcī Deī Chrīstum laudant. The friends of God praise Christ.
7. Chrīstus Deum videt. Christ sees God.
8. Deus terrās videt. God sees the earth.
9. Fīlius Deī Deum laudat. The Son of God praises God.
10. Marīa glōriam Deō dedit. Mary gave glory to God.
11. Servīs gladiōs nōn dedit. He did not give swords to the slaves.
12. Chrīstiānī rēgnum et imperium Chrīstī laudant. Christians praise the kingdom and power of Christ.

Exercise 22
1. In the town.
2. In the forest.
3. With the Gaul.
4. With Mary.
5. On account of the glory of Rome.
6. After (the) victory.
7. In the forests of Gaul.
8. With the sailor.
9. On account of the dangers of the town.
10. On earth.
11. On account of (the) victory.
12. In the gates of Rome.
13. With God.
14. On account of the rewards of the Gauls.

15. In the sky.
16. After the victory of the Romans.
17. With (the) friends.
18. In the forest.
19. In the gates of the town.
20. With the Romans.
21. In Gaul.
22. On account of the glory of war.
23. In the provinces.
24. In the province.
25. With the servant.
26. After the war.
27. With the Roman.
28. In the kingdom.
29. In the towns.
30. With the sons.
31. On account of danger.
32. In the forests and towns.
33. After the danger.
34. With Christ.
35. In war.
36. With the Christians.
37. With the Gauls.
38. On account of war.
39. Behind the town.
40. In the gate.

Exercise 23

1. Cum Marīā.
2. Post bellum.
3. Cum Deō.
4. Propter bellum.
5. In oppidō.
6. Post perīculum.
7. Propter praemium.
8. Cum Deī Fīliō.
9. Propter Chrīstiānōs.
10. In Caelō.
11. Propter rēgnum.
12. Cum amīcīs.
13. In Galliā.
14. Cum Rōmānīs.
15. Cum nautīs.
16. In silvīs.
17. In terrā.
18. In prōvinciīs.
19. Cum servō.
20. In perīculō.
21. Propter imperium.
22. Cum Gallō.
23. Post oppidum.
24. In terrā.
25. Propter Rōmae glōriam.

Exercise 24

1. "You are sons of God."
2. Christ is the Son of Mary.
3. Christians are servants of God.
4. Heaven is the reward of Christians.
5. Mary is in heaven with God.
6. The war is in the province. (There is a war in the province.)
7. We are sons of God.
8. You are a friend of God.
9. The Gauls are in Gaul, but the Romans are not in Gaul.
10. The Gauls are in the towns and in the forests.
11. The Romans did not give swords to the Gauls.
12. The forests are in Gaul. (There are forests in Gaul.)
13. Rome is not in Gaul.
14. On account of war the Gauls are not friends of the Romans.
15. The swords are in the town (There are swords in the town.)
16. You are sailors.
17. The sailors are not in the forests.
18. I am with a friend in the province.
19. The forests are behind the town.
20. The sailors are Christians.
21. We are in the town.
22. The Roman gave a reward to the servant.
23. They are friends of God.
24. You are a Christian but you are a servant of the Roman.
25. You are not in heaven.

Exercise 25

1. Chrīstus est Deī Fīlius.
2. Nautae caelum vident sed nōn terram.
3. Chrīstiānī servī Chrīstī sunt.
4. Sumus amīcī Deī.
5. Marīa cum Chrīstō in Caelō est.
6. Servī sunt in oppidīs et in silvīs.
7. Chrīstiānī Deum propter glōriam Chrīstī laudant.
8. Gallī sunt in Galliā.
9. Estis fīliī Deī.
10. Es servus Chrīstī.
11. In terrā sum.
12. Caelum est praemium servōrum Chrīstī.
13. Post bellum – praemia victōriae!
14. Rōmānī sunt in prōvinciīs.
15. Marīa est "Porta Caelī."
16. Servī sunt in oppidīs.
17. In Galliā nōn estis.

Exercise 26

On the map you see Rome and the empire of the Romans. The Romans inhabit Rome. You see the provinces of the empire of the Romans (belonging to the Roman Empire). You see Gaul. The Romans conquered the Gauls in war. The swords are not in (There are no swords in) the towns of the Gauls, because after the war the Gauls gave the swords to the Romans. And so after the victories of the Romans there is a province in Gaul. (And so after these victories there is a Roman province in Gaul.) Gauls and Romans inhabit the province. There are dangers in the forests of Gaul, because the Gauls are not friends of the Romans. The Gauls are slaves of the Romans, because the Romans conquered the Gauls. And so the Gauls do not praise the power (empire) of the Romans, but the Romans praise the power (empire) on account of the glory of war.

Exercise 27

You see Christians. You see Mary and Christ and God. The Christians are on earth, but Christ and Mary are in heaven with God. The dangers of the Christians are on earth, but the rewards are in heaven. Therefore Christians pray on earth. Mary prays with Christians because Christians are sons of Mary. Christians praise Mary because Christ is the Son of Mary. They praise Christ because He is the Son of God.

Exercise 28

The gender of the nouns listed on pages 36, 44, and 51 and the numbers of the rules in the *GRAMMAR* are as follows:

lēx, f., 50
rēx, m.., 46
dux, m., 46
lūx, f., 50
homō, m., 46
imperātor, m., 49
vēritās, f., 50
pars, f., 50
collis, m., exception to 50
hostis, m., 46
gēns, f., 50
caedēs, f., 50
flūmen, n., 51
iter, n., exception to 49
corpus, n., 52
vulnus, n., 52
agmen, n., 51
nōmen, n., 51

Exercise 29

Like lēx: frāter, frātris; pater, patris; māter, mātris; clāmor, clāmōris; prīnceps, prīncipis.
Like pars: collis, collis; hostis, hostis; gēns gentis; caedēs, caedis; mōns, montis.

Exercise 30

1. Lēx, f., No. 50;
    rēx, m., No. 46;
    dux, m., No. 46;
    lūx, f., No. 50;
    homō, m., No. 46;
    imperātor, m., No. 46;
    vēritās, f., No. 50.
2. homo, hominis, homini, hominem, homine, homines, hominum, hominibus, homines, hominibus
    imperator, imperatoris, imperatori, imperatorem, imperatore, imperatores, imperatorum, imperatoribus
    imperatores, imperatoribus
    veritas, veritatis, veritati, veritatem, veritate,
    Rex, lex, and dux – see No. 57 in grammar
3. As follows,
    (a) Lēgum
    (b) ducum
    (c) rēgum
    (d) hominum
    (e) imperātōrum
    None have the characteristics noted in Nos. 60-61.

Exercise 31

1. dat., abl. Pl., to/for the laws, by/with/from the laws.
2. gen., Pl., of the kings
3. dat., S., to/for the general
4. gen., Pl., of the leaders
5. abl. S., by/with/from the light
6. nom., acc., Pl. leaders
7. dat., S. to/for the truth
See Grammar, No. 57 for remaining answers.

Exercise 32

1. The light of truth.
2. King of kings.
3. King of men.
4. The law of God.
5. King of Christians.
6. On account of the law of God.
7. With the king.
8. On account of the truth.

Exercise 33
1. Post rēgem.
2. Hominibus.
3. Lūx vēritātis.
4. Imperātōrī.
5. Propter lēgem Chrīstī.
6. Cum duce Gallōrum.

Exercise 34
1. Christ is the King of Kings.
2. Men see the light.
3. Sailors are men. *(Hominēs* is a predicate noun.)
4. Christians praise the truth of Christ.
5. There is no light in the forests.
6. Romans do not praise the law and truth of Christ.
7. The commanders in chief of the Romans conquered the Gauls.
8. The leaders of the Gauls do not praise the law and power of the Romans.
9. Christ is King of men because He is God.
10. The leader of the Romans is in Gaul because the war is in Gaul (because there is a war in Gaul). (*Quod* is used here as a conjunction which joins a subordinate clause to a main clause.)
11. The Romans gave rewards to the commander in chief and the leaders because they conquered the Gauls. (*Ducibus* is the dative of indirect object.)
12. The Romans conquered the leaders and kings of the Gauls.

Exercise 35
1. Imperātor ducēs Gallōrum nōn laudat.
2. Chrīstus lūx hominum est quod vēritātem hominibus dedit.
3. Gallī lēgēs Rōmānōrum nōn laudant.
4. Chrīstus est Rēx Rēgum.
5. Ducēs Rōmānōrum sunt in Galliā. Itaque rēgēs Gallōrum servī Rōmānōrum sunt.
6. Imperātor perīcula bellī videt.

Exercise 36
1. The Gauls did not give rewards to Caesar, the commander in chief of the Romans.
2. The slave heard the voice of Caesar, the commander in chief.
3. God, the King of heaven and earth, gave salvation to men.
4. Caesar, the leader of the Romans, heard the voices of the Gauls in the forests.
5. For the sake of (on account of) the salvation of men Christ is man.
6. Christ, the Son of God, is the Son of Mary.

7. The Gauls, slaves of the Romans, do not praise the Romans.
8. Christians praise Christ, the Son of Mary.

Box, page 40
Saint John, the servant of Christ, heard the voice of Christ: "I am the Way and the Truth and the Life."

Excrcise 37
The words to be completed are:
1. Rēx.
2. Filiō.
3. Imperātor.
4. Fīliī.
5. Imperātōrem.
The translations:
1. Christ, the King of men, is in heaven.
2. Tile salvation of men is in Christ, the Son of God.
3. Caesar, the commander in chief of the Romans, is in Gaul.
4. The voice of Christ, the Son of God, is the voice of God.
5. The Romans praise Caesar, the commander in chief.

Exercise 38
1. Chrīstus, Fīlius Deī, est homō propter salūtem hominum.
2. Vōcem Chrīstī, Fīliī Marīae, audīvit.
3. Chrīstus, Fīlius Deī, est Rēx Rēgum.
4. Deus Chrīstō, amīcō hominum, rēgnum dedit.
5. Chrīstiānī Chrīstum, Rēgem et amīcum hominum, laudant.
6. Caesar, imperātor Rōmānōrum, vōcēs Gallōrum audīvit.
7. Propter salūtem prōvinciae Caesar, imperātor, est in Galliā.

Exercise 39
1. Porta.
2. Silva.
3. Gladius.
4. Rēx.
5. Homō.
6. Oppidum.

Exercise 40
1. gen., Pl.; of the emperors
2. gen., Pl.; of the Romans
3. acc., S.; friend
4. nom., acc., S.; danger
5. gen., Pl.; of the kings
6. nom., acc., S.; kingdom
7. acc., S.; truth
8. acc., S.; Christ

9. gen., Pl.; of the men
10. dat., S.; to/for the leader
11. gen., S.; of the friend; nom., Pl.; friends
12. dat., S; to/for the man
13. dat., abl., Pl.; to/for the sons; by/with/from the sons
14. dat., abl., Pl.; to/for the wars; by/with/from the wars
15. gen., S.; of the light
16. gen. S.; of the law

Box, page 43
The voice of the people is the voice of God.

Exercise 41
1. There are dangers in the forests of Gaul.
2. There is no peace in Gaul because Caesar is in Gaul with soldiers.
3. There are roads in the province.
4. The people praise the leader of the soldiers on account of (his) courage.
5. The Romans constructed roads in the province.
6. There is peace in heaven.
7. There are Christians in heaven.
8. In peace and in war Christians pray.
9. There are soldiers on the road.
10. Caesar gave the soldiers the rewards of courage because they conquered the Gauls.
11. The leaders of the Gauls fortified the towns.

Exercise 42
1. Sunt viae in Galliā.
2. Est bellum in prōvinciā.
3. Sunt mīlitēs in silvā.
4. Rōmānī viās mūnīvērunt.
5. Nōn est pāx in Galliā quod Caesar et mīlitēs in Galliā sunt.
6. Propter virtūtem mīlitum pāx in prōvinciā est.
7. Propter perīculum populī oppida mūnīvērunt.
8. Chrīstus est Via et Vēritās.
9. Virtūtem populī laudant.

Exercise 43
1. pars, Feminine, SOX; collis, Masculine, exception to SOX rule; hostis, common gender. Words that can indicate either males or females are designated common gender. In this text hostis is usually masculine. Gens, Feminine, SOX; caedes, Feminine, SOX.
2. partium, collium, hostium, gentium, caedium
3. pars, partis, parti, partem, parte, partes, partium, partibus, partes, partibus
   hostis, hostis, hosti, hostem, hoste, hostes, hostium, hostibus, hostes, hostibus
   gens, gentis, genti, gentem, gente, gentes, gentium, gentibus, gentes, gentibus

Box, page 45
The peace of Christ in the kingdom of Christ.

Exercise 44
1. pars, nom., S.; hostium, gen., Pl.; part of the enemy
2. caedem, acc., S.; gentium, gen., Pl.; on account of the slaughter of the tribes
3. abl., Pl.; with the enemies
4. abl. S., on the hill
5. caedem, acc.,S.; Gallorum, gen., Pl.; after the slaughter of the Gauls
6. oppidis, abl., Pl.; hostium, gen., Pl,; in the towns of the enemy (enemies)
7. abl., Pl.; on the hills
8. rex, nom., S.; gentium, gen., Pl.; king of the tribes
9. acc., S.; behind the hill
10. dat. or abl., Pl.; to/for the tribes, by/with/from the tribes
11. caedem, acc. S.; hostium, gen., Pl.; after the slaughter of the enemy

Exercise 45
7. Propter salūtem gentium.
8. Pars dūcum et mīlitum.
9. Cum imperātōre hostium.
10. Propter caedem hominum.
11. In colle.
12. Cum hostibus.
13. In viā.
14. Ducēs gentium.

Exercise 46
1. The leaders of the Romans conquered the enemy on a hill. (The leaders conquered the enemies of the Romans on the hill.)
2. On account of the slaughter of the soldiers there is a war in Gaul.
3. There are dangers in Gaul because the Gauls are enemies of the Romans.
4. Christ is the King of nations and the salvation of men because He is God.
5. Part of the enemy is in the forests, but part is on the hill.
6. In Gaul there are hills and forests, towns and roads.
7. The Romans conquered the kings and tribes of Gaul.
8. On account of the welfare of the people and the peace of the provinces the Romans constructed roads.
9. Men praise courage and truth.
10. After the slaughter of the enemy Caesar praises the soldiers for (on account of) their courage.

Exercise 47

1. Pars hostium, in oppidīs est, sed pars in colle est.
2. Propter caedem ducum gentis, Gallī Caesarem nōn laudant.
3. Chrīstus est Rēx gentium et populōrum.
4. Sunt collēs post oppidum.
5. Post victōriam est caedēs partis ducum gentis.
6. Pars hostium in collibus et in silvīs est.

Exercise 48

1. The final *a* of the nominative is short, of the ablative, long.
2. *nauta*, masculine, natural gender, No. 46; *praemium*, neuter; *lex*, feminine, SOX, No. 50; *homo*, masculine, natural gender, No. 46; *Christus*, masculine, natural gender, No. 46; *veritas*, feminine, SOX, No. 50.
3. Christ, the Son of God, gave glory and a reward to the friends of God.
   a. Rules for cases:
      i. Fīlius, No. 473
      ii. praemium, No. 745
      iii. amīcīs, No. 737.

Exercise 49

1. See Nos. 46-52.
2. See Nos. 59-63.

Exercise 50

1. Acc. sing.

2-9. Gen. pl.

Exercise 51

1. on account of the courage of the soldiers
2. peace of the peoples and tribes
3. on account of the shouting of the enemy
4. after the slaughter of the fathers and mothers
5. on account of the light and truth of Christ
6. with the general of the Romans
7. on account of the safety of the brothers
8. on the hill
9. on the mountains
10. after the leader
11. with the king
12. the voices of the men
13. with part of the soldiers
14. with Caesar

Exercise 52

1. You Are Brothers. Christ is the King of men but He is (also) the brother of men, and God is the King of men but He is (also) the Father of men. And so men are brothers. And so war is the slaughter of brothers. And therefore God and Christ do not praise war.
2. The Slaughter of the Gauls. The Romans killed a part of the chiefs of the Gauls. And so God

heard the shouting of mothers and of fathers and of brothers in the forests and mountains of Gaul.

3. In Gaul. There are forests and mountains and hills in Gaul. There are towns in the hills, but part of the tribes of the Gauls inhabit the mountains and forests.
4. Christ, the Leader of Men. Christ is the leader of men because He gave truth and law and light to men. Christ is the way and the truth.
5. Our Tainted Nature's Solitary Boast." Mary is the Mother of Christ. But Christ is God because He is the Son of God the Father. And so Mary is the Mother of God. Christians praise Mary, the Mother of God. Mary is mother of men because Christ on the cross gave Mary to men. And so Christians are sons and servants of Mary. Mary is the gate of heaven.

Box, page 50

I am a soldier of Christ.

Exercise 53

1. Clāmōrem prīncipum audīvit.
2. Prīncipēs gentis occīdērunt.
3. Sunt perīcula in montibus.
4. Imperātor mātrēs et patrēs mīlitum laudat.
5. Frātrēs in Galliā cum Caesare sunt.
6. Propter bellum collēs mūnīvērunt.
7. Rōmānī viās in montibus mūnivērunt.

Exercise 54

1. nom., acc., Pl., rivers
2. abl., S., on the march
3. acc., S. on account of the name
4. abl., S., gen., S., in the name of the Father
5. acc., S., gen., S., on account of the name of Christ
6. gen., Pl., of the names
7. nom., or acc., S., gen., S., the name of the Father
8. abl., S., by/with/from the name

See Grammar No. 64 for remaining answers

Exercise-55

1. In flūmine.
2. Propter vulnera.
3. In itinere.
4. In agmine.
5. In nōmine Marīae.
6. In corpore.
7. Cum agmine.
8. In itinere.
9. Post iter.
10. Nōmen flūminis.

11. Propter lēgem.
12. Cum imperātōribus
13. Salūs gentium.
14. In monte.

Exercise 56

1. On account of wounds the soldier is not in the column.
2. The general sees the soldiers' wounds.
3. There are bodies in the river.
4. There are rivers and forests in Gaul.
5. The Romans are on the march.
6. There are enemies in the forests and in the mountains. And so we are in danger.
7. Caesar sees the enemy's column.
8. Christians praise the name of Mary.
9. The enemy's column is on the river.
10. The Romans killed Christians because Christians praise the name of Christ.

Exercise 57

1. Sunt corpora et gladiī in flūmine.
2. Agmen in montibus est.
3. Chrīstiānī in nōmine Chrīstī, Fīliī Deī, ōrant.
4. Sunt frātrēs et patrēs in agmine.
5. Sunt perīcula in itinere quod hostēs in collibus sunt.
6. Post iter collem mūnīvērunt.
7. Iter in montibus est.
8. Nautae terram et caelum vident.
9. Rēx propter salūtem rēgnī ōrat.

Exercise 58

See Introduction, 3.
The genders and the grammar numbers giving the rules for the genders are:

1. nōmen, n., 51
2. rēx, m., 46
3. vēritās, f., 50
4. māter, f., 47
5. mōns, m., exception to 50
6. agmen, n., 51
7. dux, c., but in FIRST YEAR LATIN always m. because the leaders are always men
8. mīles, m., 46
9. caedēs, f., 50
10. pater, m., 46
11. flūmen, n., 51
12. clāmor, m., 49
13. lūx, f., 50
14. homō, m., 46
15. virtūs, f., 50
16. iter, n., exception to 49
17. prīnceps, m., 46
18. pars, f., 50
19. hostis, c., but in FIRST YEAR LATIN always m. because the enemies are men
20. salūs, f., 50
21. collis, m., exception to 50
22. vōx, f., 50
23. frāter, m., 46
24. corpus, n., 52
25. imperātor, m., 46, 49
26. pāx, f, 50
27. vulnus, n., 52
28. gēns, f., 50.

Exercise 59

1. "You are the light of the world."
2. Christ was in the world on account of (for) the salvation of men.
3. Christ gave light and a law, salvation and truth to men.
4. Caesar, commander in chief of the Romans, was with the soldiers in Gaul.
5. Christ is the salvation of the world.
6. The slaves praise the king's name.
7. The army of the enemy was in the mountains.
8. On account of the slaughter of the leading men there was no peace.
9. On account of wounds the soldiers were not on the march.
10. God, the Father of men, praises courage but He does not praise wars and slaughter.
11. The leader heard the cries of the slaves and the shouting of the soldiers.
12. After the war there were bodies on the hills and in the rivers, and the commander in chief heard the shouting of mothers.
13. Christians are Christ's brothers and Christ's soldiers.
14. The Romans killed a part of the leading men of the Gauls.
15. The tribes and peoples of Gaul do not praise the power of the Romans.

Exercise 60

1. In nōmine rēgis.
2. Propter salūtem hominum.
3. In itinere.
4. In montibus et in collibus.
5. Cum prīncipibus gentium.
6. Lūcem, mundī vident.
7. Post caedem ducum.
8. Erant corpora in viā.
9. Propter virtūtem mīlitis.

10. Virtūtēs Christiānōrum laudat.
11. In pāce et in bellō.
12. Vōcem imperātōris audīvit.
13. Partem hostium occīdērunt.
14. Lēgēs gentis laudant.
15. Caesar praemia mīlitibus dedit.
16. Propter vulnera prīncipum.
17. Imperātor clāmōrem pātrum audīvit.
18. Agmen in flūmine erat.
19. Mātrēs agmen vident.
20. Propter salūtem gentis.
21. Vōcēs frātrum audīvit.
22. Deus vēritātem hominibus dedit.
23. Propter salūtem agminis.
24. In itinere.
25. Erat iter in montibus.
26. Caesar gladiōs prīncipī nōn dedit.
27. Gallī praemium imperātōrī dedērunt.

Exercise 61
1. Chrīstus est Fīlius Deī.
2. Marīa Māter Deī et hominum est.
3. Mīles in colle est.
4. Mīles agmen hostium videt.
5. Servī viam mūnīvērunt.
6. Rōmānī Chrīstiānōs occīdērunt.

Exercise 62
See No. 65., Grammar

Exercise 63
1. after the coming of Christ
2. the coming of Caesar
3. in the harbor
4. the harbor of the province
5. with the cavalry
6. in the army
7. after the cavalry
8. of the army, or armies
9. in the Senate
10. in the province
11. the Senate
12. the law of the Senate
13. on account of fear
14. the friends of the Senate
15. fear of Caesar
16. an attack
17. leader of the cavalry
18. with the army

Exercise 64
1. Propter metum perīculī.
2. In senātū.
3. Cum exercitū Caesaris.
4. Post adventum Chrīstī.
5. Cum equitātū Gallōrum.
6. Impetus hostium.
7. Cum spīritū Deī.
8. In portū.

Exercise 65
1. Now there are harbors in Gaul. (Abl.; no idea of motion)
2. After the coming of the Romans there was war in Gaul.
3. Caesar came into the province with the cavalry. (Acc.; motion toward.)
4. Caesar, however, was not with the army.
5. On account of fear of the Romans the Gauls came into the forests.
6. The sailors see the harbor.
7. The Senate praises Caesar because the Romans conquered the enemy.
8. They made an attack against the enemy.
9. After the arrival of the cavalry the soldiers made an attack against the Gauls.
10. The Gauls were on the hill. Caesar's soldiers, however, made an attack against the Gauls. They killed the leaders and chiefs of the Gauls and conquered the Gauls. After the war, on account of fear of Caesar, the enemy did not make an attack against the Romans.
11. The Gauls killed the senate.

Exercise 66
1. dat., abl., Pl., to/for, by/with/from the harbors
2. gen., S., nom., acc., Pl., of the harbor, harbors
3. nom., S., body
4. abl., S., by/with/from the calvary
5. abl., S., by/with/from the spirit
6. acc., S., harbor
7. acc., S., gate
8. gen., Pl., of the harbors
9. gen., Pl., of the gates
10. acc., S., attack
11. gen., Pl., of the kings
12. acc., S., fear

Exercise 67
The Slaughter of the Christians.
After the coming of Christ the light of truth was in the world but the Romans were not friends of Christ and of truth. The Christians, however, were friends of Christ. There were many Christians in the empire of the Romans. They were in the harbors and in the towns of the provinces and in the forests and in the mountains. They were in the army and in the cavalry and in the Senate. They were slaves and soldiers; they were

mothers and fathers, Gauls and Romans. On account of fear of Christ the King, however, and on account of the name of the Christians' God, the Romans killed the Christians. After the slaughter of the Christians the Romans were not friends and servants of God. The Christians, however, because the Romans killed the Christians on account of the law of Christ, are now in heaven with Mary and Christ and see the glory of God the father.

1. The light of truth.
2. No.
3. Yes.
4. In the harbors, towns, forests, and mountains; in the army, cavalry, and Senate.
5. Slaves and soldiers, mothers and fathers, Gauls and Romans.
6. They killed them.

Exercise 68

The Conquest of Gaul.

Gallī nōn erant amīcī Caesaris et senātūs. Itaque Caesar in Galliam cum equitātū et mīlitibus vēnit. Gallī autem, propter metum Caesaris, in silvās et in montēs vēnērunt. Exercitus Caesaris in silvīs hostium erat, et perīcula erant. Rōmānī autem in hostēs impetum fēcērunt. Ducēs et prīncipēs Gallōrum occīdērunt. Equitātum et exercitum Gallōrum vīcērunt, et portūs et oppida et collēs Galliae mūnīvērunt. Itaque senātus propter glōriam bellī et virtūtem mīlitum, Caesarem nunc laudat. Propter metum mīlitum Gallī nunc amīcī et servī senātūs sunt.

Exercise 69

God Is Everywhere. "God is a spirit." He is in heaven and on earth. He sees the world. He sees, men. He sees the soldiers and the sailors and the servants. He sees the mothers and the fathers, the brothers and the sons. He praises men on account of virtue (courage), but He does not praise (them) on account of slaughter.

Exercise 70

acies, aciei, aciei, aciem, acie, acies, acierum, aciebus, acies, aciebus

spes, spei spei, spem, spe

fides, fidei, fidei, fidem, fide

Exercise 71

1. in the battle line
2. on account of faith
3. to/for, by/with/from things
4. on account of hope
5. on account of the affair
6. by/with, from the thing
7. of the things
8. behind the battle line
9. to/for, by/with/from battle lines

Exercise 72

1. The soldiers were in battle line.
2. The Romans killed the Christians on account of the (their) faith.
3. The soldiers placed hope of victory in courage.
4. The Romans made an attack against the enemy's battle line.
5. The Gauls see the battle line of the Romans on the hill.
6. In Christ is the hope of the world.
7. God praises Christians on account of faith and virtue.
8. The soldiers see the affair.

Exercise 73

1. Caesar in aciē erat.
2. Fidem mīlitis laudant.
3. Senātus rem nōn laudat.
4. Gallī in aciem Rōmānōrum impetum fēcērunt.
5. Spem in Deō posuērunt.

Exercise 74

1.
Hostium	declined like *pars*, No. 60
virtūtum	regular
hominum	regular
gentium	like *pars*, No. 61.

2.
Homō	m.	No. 46
rēs	f.	No. 70
nauta	m.	No. 32
māter	f.	No. 47
vēritās	f.	No. 50
pax	f.	No. 50
gēns	f.	No. 50
servus	m.	No. 35
equitātus	m.	No. 66
praemium	n.	No. 38
Rōmānus	m.	No. 35

Exercise 75

1. Chrīstiānī propter cōpiam grātiae Chrīstī Deō grātiās agunt.
2. Propter metum Caesaris gentēs in castra impetum nōn fēcērunt.
3. Erat cōpia gladiōrum in castrīs.
4. Imperātor propter victōriam in grātiā cum rēge erat.
5. In castra impetum fēcērunt.
6. Cōpiae hostium in prōvincīā nōn erant.
7. Spem in grātiā Chrīstī posuērunt.
8. Propter caedem prīncipum bellum erat in Galliā. Caesar in Galliam cum cōpiīs et

equitātū et impedīmentīs vēnit. Cōpiae hostium in colle erant. Rōmānī autem post collem castra posuērunt. Gallī propter metum Caesaris in castra impetum nōn fēcērunt. Rōmānī autem in Gallōs impetum fēcērunt. Gallī in equitātū spem posuērunt, sed Rōmānī equitātum Gallōrum occīdērunt et collem cēpērunt. Ducēs et castra et impedīmenta Gallōrum cēpērunt. Post bellum erat pāx in Galliā et Rōmānī in prōvinciam venērunt.

Exercise 76
The Camp of the Romans.
You see the army of the Romans in camp. You see soldiers and leaders and the commander in chief. You see the soldiers' swords. You do not see the baggage, but the baggage is in the camp. There is an abundance of all things in the camp. The soldiers pitched camp on a hill but not in the forest. The battle line came into the camp with the baggage train. The enemy, however, made an attack against the camp, but the troops of the Romans conquered the enemy. Now the commander in chief praises the soldiers and the leaders on account of (their) courage and the leaders give thanks to the soldiers on account of the victory. On account of the victory the commander in chief came into favor with the Senate.

Exercise 77
"Woe to the Conquered!"
The Gauls were enemies of the Romans. Therefore the Romans came into Gaul with troops and pitched camp. In the camp there were soldiers and cavalry and slaves and the soldiers' baggage. There was an abundance of swords in the camp. There were battle lines on the hills, in the mountains, and in the forest. The Gauls made an attack against the Romans; the Romans, however, made an attack against the Gauls. The Romans placed hope of victory in courage; the Gauls placed hope of safety in courage. The Romans, however, conquered the Gauls. They killed part (some) of the leading men (chiefs) and the leaders of the Gauls; they captured the harbors and towns of the Gauls. And so the Gauls gave an abundance of swords and slaves to the Romans. After the war there was peace in Gaul, but there were camps of the Romans in Gaul and the Gauls were slaves of the Romans. The commander in chief of the Romans was Caesar. The Senate praises Caesar and the army on account of the victory and the courage of the soldiers, and the Romans give thanks to Caesar.

Exercise 78
Brothers in Christ. On account of the grace of God we are Christians. And therefore we are brothers on account of the law of Christ: "You are brothers."

Exercise 79
Castra. Mōns (silva). Mīles. Via. Senātus. Portus. Agmen. Impedīmenta. Aciēs. Equitātus. Lēx. Imperātor (dux). Collis. Flūmen.

Exercise 80
Who Is Christ? Christ, the Son of God, is the son of Mary. Therefore He is man and God. Christ is King of men because He is God. In Christ is man's salvation because, on account of the salvation of men, He came into the world. He is the "Light of the World" because He gave men truth. And so Christians give thanks to God and to Christ, and praise Christ, King and Commander.

Exercise 81
The genders and the GRAMMAR numbers giving the rules for the genders are:
1. n. 52
2. m. 35
3. f. 70
4. f. 50
5. f. 33
6. n. 51
7. m. 46
8. f. 33
9. n. 38
10. f. 33
11. n. 52
12. n. 38
13. c. but here m. by 46
14. n. 51
15. m. 35
16. f. 47
17. n. 51
18. n. 38
19. m. 35
20. m. 46
21. n. exception to 49
22. c. but here m. by 46
23. f. 33
24. f. 50
25. m. 46
26. m. 35
27. f. 33
28. m. exception to 50
29. m. 35
30. m. exception to 50
31. f. 33;

32. m. 46
33. m. 35
34. c. but here m. by 46
35. m. 35
36. n. 38
37. f. 50
38. f. 50
39. m. 32
40. f. 33
41. m. 46
42. m. 35
43. f. 50
44. m. 66

Exercise 82

The genders and the grammar numbers giving the rules
for the genders are:
1. f. 50
2. m. 46
3. f. 70
4. m. 35
5. m. 35
6. m. 66
7. m. 66
8. f. 33
9. m. 66
10. f. 50
11. f. 70
12. m. 66
13. f. 50
14. f. 50
15. f. 70
16. m. 49

Exercise 83

1. God, the father of men, is in heaven.
2. God gave a law to men. *(Hominibus,* dat.,
   indirect object.)
3. On account of (For The sake of) men's
   salvation Christ was man on earth.
4. Christ is the light of the world. (*Lūx,* predicate
   noun.)
5. Christ, the Son of God, is King of tribes and
   peoples. (*Fīlius,* appositive.)
6. After the coming of Christ there was truth in
   the world. *(Adventum,* acc. after *post.)*
7. The spirit of God was in Christ.
8. The kingdom of Christ is the kingdom of
   heaven.
9. Christians pray in the name of Christ.
10. Mary, with Christ in the kingdom of heaven,
    now sees the glory of God. *(Rēgnō,* abl. after
    in, no motion expressed.)

11. Mary, the Mother of God, is the gate of
    heaven.
12. Heaven is the reward of virtue.
13. God praises the faith of Christians. *(Fidem,*
    direct object.)
14. You are brothers.
15. A friend is the servant of a (his) friend.
16. Soldiers praise peace.
17. Rome is not in Gaul, but there is a province of
    the Romans in Gaul.
18. The Gauls inhabit Gaul.
19. The sailors see the harbors.
20. The Romans constructed roads in the
    provinces.
21. Christians do not praise the slaughter of the
    enemy's leading men.
22. Caesar did not give the command of Gaul to
    the Gauls.
23. The commander in chief heard the shouting
    and cries of the enemy.
24. On account of wounds the soldiers did not
    make the march.
25. On account of (Through) fear the leader
    praises the king.
26. On account of war there were soldiers and a
    supply of swords in the town. *(Erant* agrees
    with *mīlitēs et cōpia;* see No. 471.)
27. The enemy was-in the mountains and on the
    hills.
28. The bodies of the soldiers were in the forest.
29. They killed a part of the cavalry in the river.
30. The Senate and the leading men give thanks to
    the army on account of the victory. *(Exercituī,*
    indirect object.)
31. The Romans placed hope in courage.
32. Caesar came into camp with troops and
    baggage.
33. On account of the influence of Caesar the
    leading men of the Gauls gave slaves to the
    Romans.
34. The enemy was behind the Romans' battle
    line. The cavalry, however, came into the
    battle line. And so the Romans conquered and
    killed the enemy. *(Aciem* acc. after *in,*
    expressing motion toward.)
35. Caesar came into the forests of Gaul. The
    leading men of the Gauls, however, saw the
    affair. They therefore made an attack against
    Caesar's battle line.
36. Soldiers in battle line pray because they are in
    danger.

Exercise 84

1. In the deep river.
2. With a great army.
3. After the great war.
4. With holy Mary.
5. On a long road.
6. With good men.
7. With large forces.
8. With many soldiers.
9. In great danger.
10. In high mountains.
11. With a good man.
12. After a long march.
13. On account of many wounds.
14. With a bad servant.

Exercise 85

1. Cum multīs mīlitibus.
2. In altīs montibus.
3. Propter lēgem sānctam Deī.
4. Cum homine bonō.
5. Magna corpora.
6. Cum prīmīs Chrīstiānīs.
7. Lēgēs malae.
8. Alta flūmina.
9. Longa via.
10. Propter magnum metum Rōmānōrum.
11. Magnus clāmor.
12. Sāncta Marīa.

Exercise 86

1. Many Christians were in the first battle line. (Abl. after *in*, no motion expressed.)
2. Holy Mary prays.
3. A long column came into the high mountains. (Acc. after *in*, expressing motion toward.)
4. The bad sailor does not pray.
5. A good leader praises the great courage of the soldiers. (*Bonus*, adj. of quality follows noun; *magnam*, adj. of quantity precedes noun.)
6. In a long column there are many soldiers and much baggage.

Exercise 87

1. Ducēs bonī pācem laudant.
2. Rēgēs malī multōs Chrīstiānōs occīdērunt.
3. Longum agmen in silvīs erat, sed prīma aciēs in altīs montibus erat.
4. Propter magnam glōriam Rōmae multī hominēs lēgēs Rōmānōrum laudant.
5. Sunt magnī montēs et alta flūmina in Americā.
6. Chrīstiānī servī sānctae Marīae sumus.

Exercise 88

1. Angusta.
2. Bonus.
3. Tūtī.
4. Rōmāna.
5. Chrīstiānī.
6. Malae.
7. Reliqua.
8. Sānctī.
9. Altum.
10. Prīmī.
11. Sānctus.
12. Multae.
13. Tūtī.
14. Magnī.
15. Malus.
16. Longa.
17. Sānctus.
18. Tūtī.

Box, page 77

The welfare of the people is the highest law. Let the welfare of the people be the highest law.

Box, page 78

Glory be to the Father, and to the Son, and to the Holy Spirit

Exercise 89

1. The Roman legions were in front of (before) the camp.
2. Holy Mary prays for bad men and for good men.
3. Many Gauls were before the gates of the camp.
4. The leading men were in front of a high wall.
5. The Roman soldiers pitched camp in front of (before) the wall of the large town.
6. Christians pray for (their) friends.
7. On behalf of the good king the soldiers made an attack against the enemy.
8. There was a great scarcity of grain in Gaul.
9. The rest of the Christian soldiers were in the first battle line before the forest.
10. Slaves praise a good master.

Exercise 90

There was a great scarcity of grain in the Roman camp because the Gauls did not give a supply of grain to the Romans and there were no crops in Gaul. The Gauls were not friends of the Romans. Caesar, therefore, came into Gaul with troops and baggage. Caesar's column was long. The road was in (ran through) narrow and high mountains. The Gauls therefore made an attack against the long column, but the Roman legions conquered the Gauls. And so the remaining Gauls came into a safe city. The Romans, however, pitched camp before the high wall. Caesar's first battle line was in front of the camp. The Gauls, however, on account of (their) great fear of Caesar, did not make an attack against the Roman camp. And so the Romans made an attack against the Gauls and conquered the Gauls. They killed many Gauls and a great part of Gaul's leading men. After Caesar's victory there was peace in Gaul. And so the Gauls gave the Romans a large supply of grain, and there was no scarcity of grain in the Roman camp.

Box, page 79
Holy, holy, holy, Lord God of hosts (armies).

Exercise 91
1. Prō magnīs castrīs altum flūmen est.
2. Mūrī oppidī sunt altī.
3. Caesar erat magnus imperātor.
4. Erat magna inopia frūmentī.
5. Erant multae legiōnēs cum Caesare in Galliā.
6. Sāncta Marīa prō hominibus ōrat.
7. Chrīstus Dominus prō mundō ōrat.
8. Servī Rōmānī dominōs nōn laudant.
9. Sunt magna frūmenta in Galliā.

Exercise 92
1. The column was long. (*Longum,* predicate adjective; nom. sing., n., with *agmen.*)
2. The remaining Gauls were not safe. (*Reliquī,* nom. pl., m., with *Gallī*; adj. of quantity precedes noun.)
3. On behalf of the good commander in chief the Christian soldiers made an attack against the enemy. (*Chrīstiānī,* nom. pl., m., with *mīlitēs*; adj. of quality follows noun. *Bonō,* abl. sing., m., with *imperātōre*; adj. of quality follows noun.)
4. The road was narrow. (Forms of *sum* may stand anywhere.)
5. The long column came into the high mountains. (*Longum,* nom. sing., n., with *agmen*; adj. of quantity precedes noun.)
6. The first legion was in battle line. (*Prīma,* nom. sing., f., with *legiō*; adj. of quantity precedes noun.)
7. There was a great scarcity of grain in the remaining tribes. (*Magna,* nom. sing., f., with *inopia*; adj. of quantity precedes noun. *Reliquīs,* abl. pl., f, with *gentibus*; adj. of quantity precedes noun.)

8. Bad men do not pray for the rest of the men. (*Malī,* nom. pl., m., with *hominēs*; adj. of quality follows noun.)
9. There are many rivers in Gaul. (*Multa,* nom. pl., n., with *flūmina*; adj. of quantity precedes noun.)
10. The master, a good and holy man, gave grain to the servants. (*Bonus,* nom. sing., m., with *homō*; adj. of quality follows noun.)
11. The Roman legions were in battle line before the high wall. (*Altō,* abl. sing., m., with *mūrō*; adj. of quantity generally, but not always, precedes noun.)

Box, page 80
In the name of the Lord.

Exercise 93
1. Malās.
2. Bonīs.
3. Magnum.
4. Magnā.
5. Rōmānō.
6. Bonīs.
7. Multīs.
8. Chrīstiānam.
9. Magnam.
10. Rōmāna.
11. Longā.
12. Magnum.

Box, Page 81
The earth is the Lord's! Great is the glory of the Lord!

Exercise 94
1. With Caesar, the Roman general,
2. On account of the welfare of the Roman people.
3. In the high mountains.
4. After a great slaughter.
5. On account of many wounds.
6. On account of the welfare of the remaining tribes.
7. For the holy name.
8. In the deep river.

Exercise 95
1. See No. *78.*
2. See No. 78.
3. (1) Homine fortī, hominēs fortēs, hominum fortium.
   (2) Omnī Chrīstiānō, omnēs Chrīstiānī, omnium Chrīstiānōrum.

(3) Duce nōbilī, ducēs nōbilēs, ducum nōbilium.

(4) Brevī itinere, brevia itinera, brevium itinerum.

(5) Viā difficilī, viae difficilēs, viārum difficilium.

(6) Bellō gravī, bella gravia, bellōrum gravium.

4. (1) Salūtem commūnem, salūte commūnī.
(2) Omnem Galliam, omnī Galliā.
(3) Rem gravem, rē gravī.
(4) Metum gravem, metū gravī.
(5) Oppidum nōbile, oppidō nōbilī.
(6) Omnem spem, omnī spē.
(7) Vulnus grave, vulnere gravī.
(8) Viam facilem, viā facilī.
(9) Nōmen nōbile, nōmine nōbilī.

5. (a) Difficilī. On a different route.
(b) Omnibus. With all the troops.
(c) Nōbilī. For a noble king.
(d) Fortī. For a brave friend.
(e) Nōbilī. For a noble (renowned) leader.
(f) Grave. After a severe war.
(g) Gravem. On account of severe fear.
(h) Omnī. With all the cavalry.
(i) Fortibus. With the brave soldiers.
(j) Gravia. On account of serious wounds.
(k) Commūnem. On account of the common welfare.
(1) Nōbile. Behind the renowned town.

Exercise 96

1. Fortis, nōbilis. Christ the Lord, King of men, was strong and noble.
2. Brevis. The hope of the Gauls was short.
3. Nōbilis. The renowned leader was in the first battle line.
4. Fortēs. Before the camp there were brave soldiers.
5. Omnem. They placed all hope of safety in courage.
6. Omnem. Christians place all hope of salvation in the name of Christ.
7. Gravem. On account of a serious affair Caesar came into Gaul.
8. Commūnem. On account of the common welfare all the Gauls made an attack against the province.
9. Difficilis. On account of the mountains and forests the route was difficult.

10. Facilis. On account of the courage of the Gauls the thing was not easy.

Exercise 97

1. Perīculum erat grave.
2. Estis fortēs.
3. Propter salūtem commūnem hominum Chrīstus in mundum vēnit.
4. Via erat difficilis.
5. Omnēs hominēs magnam virtūtem laudant.
6. Erant mīlitēs fortēs et ducēs nōbilēs in exercitū Rōmānō.
7. Iter nōn erat facile.
8. Montēs magnī et altī sunt.
9. Omnis imperātor virtūtem et fidem laudat.
10. Caesar imperātor magnus et nōbilis erat.
11. Victōria nōn erat facilis.
12. Iter erat breve.
13. Gladiī Rōmānī erant gravēs.
14. Rēs erat gravis.
15. Chrīstus dominus nōbilis et dux fortis est. Itaque omnēs hominēs bonī et sānctī Chrīstum Dominum, laudant.
16. Lēgēs Rōmānae erant gravēs.
17. Flūmina longa et alta Americae sunt nōbilia.

Exercise 98

1. The Gauls were eager for fame.
2. The son is like the father.
3. The Gauls were next to (were the tribe living nearest to) the province.
4. Mary is full of grace.
5. Gaul was full of Romans.
6. The town was full of soldiers and of swords.
7. The province is full of all good things.
8. Heaven is full of the glory of God.
9. We are eager for all good things.
10. They were next to Gaul (lived nearer to Gaul than any others).
11. Holy men are like Christ.

Exercise 99

1. Gladiōrum (gladiīs).
2. Victōriae.
3. Galliae.
4. Rōmānōrum. (Rōmānīs).
5. Fīnitimārum.
6. Mīlitis (mīlitī).
7. Bellī.

Box, page 88
All for Jesus.

Exercise 100

The name of Jesus is the (a) holy name. It is a name noble and full of hope. All Christians pray in the name of Jesus; all praise Jesus; all give thanks to Jesus; all in heaven, with Mary see Jesus. In Jesus' name the first Christians conquered the Romans. On account of Jesus, God the Father gave the first Christians the reward of victory. And so Jesus Christ is both Lord and King of all men.

Exercise 101

1. Christians praise both Jesus Christ and Mary.
2. Rome is a city both great and renowned.
3. Caesar was eager for both fame and power.
4. At dawn the brave cavalry made an attack against the rest of the enemy.
5. On account of serious dangers and the soldiers' many wounds the Romans made a short march into the province.

Exercise 102

What do you see in the picture? In the picture you see a Roman column. It is a long column, but you see a part of the column. You see the standards of the legion and the swords of the soldiers. Part of the column is on the bridge. The cavalry, however, is not on the bridge. You see the commander in chief. He comes first. There is a baggage train in the column. In the baggage train is a supply of grain and of all things. You see the city and the high wall.

Exercise 103

1. Sunt multī pontēs in flūminibus longīs et altīs in Americā.
2. Mīlitēs Rōmānī propter nōmen Jēsū multōs Chrīstīanōs occīdērunt.
3. In Americā oppida magna et nōbilia sunt.
4. Chrīstiānī omnem spem et fidem in Dominō Jēsū Chrīstō posuērunt.
5. Et nautae et mīlitēs Deum laudant.
6. Urbs Rōma magna et nōbilis est.
7. Prīmā lūce imperātor signum dedit. Itaque equitēs in hostēs impetum fēcērunt et magnam partem, prīncipum gentis occīdērunt.
8. Vidētis signa legiōnum.
9. Vulnera mīlitum fortium sunt multa et gravia.
10. Hostēs equitem Rōmānum occīdērunt.
11. Pontēs mūnīvērunt.
12. Quid Chrīstiānī laudant?

Box, page 90

The Sign of the Cross. In the name of the Father and of the Son and of the Holy Spirit. Amen.

Reading No. 3

What is victory? It is the reward of courage. What is war? It is the slaughter of brothers. What is a soldier? He is the bulwark of empire.